All My Favourite People Are Broken

All My Favourite People Are Broken

For Serno —
If this ever gets optioned, you're my guy
Best,
[signature]

Brent Jensen

Author of **NO SLEEP 'TIL SUDBURY** and **LEFTOVER PEOPLE**

EDWARDS PRESS COMPANY
TORONTO

Edwards Press Company

ALL MY FAVOURITE PEOPLE ARE BROKEN Copyright ©2015 by Brent Jensen. All rights reserved. Printed in the United States of America. No part of this book may be used or reproduced in any manner whatsoever without written permission except in the case of brief quotations embodied in critical articles and reviews.

FIRST EDITION

ISBN 13: 9780987715920

Copyright © 2015 Brent Jensen

All rights reserved.

ISBN: 0987715925

For one of my best friends, Dr. Liam Ennis
"So good for fixin' anything that I got broken"

Foreword

My old pal Garvey and I have been talking about the importance of music in our lives forever. That's in *our* lives, to be clear. People will have differing inclinations when it comes to their own personal valuation of music and what it means to them, if anything.

Most people understood what we were trying to do when we explained to them the adventure upon which we were about to embark. They got it. You could tell they got it when their eyes lit up halfway through the explanation.

If it unfolded in the way I hoped it would, this would serve as the culmination of discussions we'd had late at night in dimly lit spaces across North America as long as we'd known each other - hunched over our guitars, ribbons of cigarette smoke rising up from overflowing ashtrays to further fortify the dense blue air wavering gently above our heads, empty bottles of Stoli and Moosehead and Miller Lite and whatever else lying about. This setting never failed to give rise to lengthened deliberations about our favourite songs and musical heroes, and how intensely liberated we felt by the power they lent. That beautiful communion it would consistently afford us.

And now, through this proposed exercise, it would be time to directly assess the emotional investment we had made in the music we most cherished over the course of our lives.

The rules were pretty simple: there would be no formality. No 'lists', no rankings. Nice and loose. We would both individually gather up all of the music that ever made us *feel* something, and hole ourselves up together in a completely isolated area to take a closer look inside it all, for however long it took. There would be no boundaries in terms of musical genre, or structure of any description - the landscape was wide open. If a melody from a commercial jingle floated your boat for whatever reason, it had to be included.

Given the scope of this undertaking, I could never really be certain of what would actually result from it. But I had a good idea of what I was looking for. And after my plane ticket was purchased, my excitement to carry it out could barely be restrained.

If your eyes lit up as you read this, even just a bit - keep reading. You get it.

CHAPTER 1

New York State of Mind

"I just saw Springsteen on *The Tonight Show*. The guy's a king, I love him," I texted Garvey. The Boss was one of his musical heroes growing up. Mine were Ace Frehley and Nikki Sixx.

His response appeared a minute later on my iPhone.

"We need to sit down, get comfortably numb, and wag our chins soon."

"Indeed," I responded. "Been thinking about going out that way to do some promotion, but I have something planned for Southern California soon that may prevent me from getting there. It's on my mind though, and I'll get there eventually."

I don't call it SoCal for the same reasons I don't refer to Scarlett Johansson as 'ScarJo'.

Garvey lived out in western Canada, having moved there years ago to set up shop after obtaining his doctorate in forensic psychology in the southern United States. We had both completed our undergrad thesis studies together up in Sudbury twenty years ago this May, and though our life paths diverged, we didn't allow for geography or the passing of time to get in the way. We still saw each other every couple of years be it in Edmonton, Toronto, or elsewhere. We talked on the phone regularly.

"You around for a call this weekend?" I texted. "I saw Joe Bonamassa downtown last weekend, and he killed. You need to hear about it. I also want to discuss this:" I attached a picture I had just taken at the local music store of the new Eddie Van Halen 'Frankenstrat' guitar replicas that Sir Edward had just released. I wanted one.

"Oh my," came back. Garv wasn't a Van Halen fan. I was rabidly so.

"We are so different, yet so much the same…" he continued.

"Listen, I'm also kicking around an idea I want to run by you," I responded.

"I'm intrigued," came the reply.

"I think we need to take some time and lock ourselves in a room together with some of our all-time favourite records, two guitars, and assorted party favours and see what comes of it. What do you say?" I asked.

"Screw the weekend. Calling you tonight," Garvey sent back.

Garvey and I discussed this little prospect in great detail that night. After we worked out what we wanted from this initial idea and approximated a general timeline, we went back and forth with this musical summit proposition, paring possibilities down from a mass of random ideas surrounding format and location. I ended up scuttling my plans to go to California.

To do this at one of our homes would be easiest. But ease and practicality weren't primary concerns. We talked about getting together in a locale known for its musicality - a Memphis, or a Nashville. Maybe Austin. After concluding that we needed to focus more on the task at hand than the cities in which we wanted to conduct ourselves like twenty-two year olds, we figured that the opposite would be more suitable. We needed to go somewhere where we could be isolated and completely focus on the music, away from distraction. Since Garvey was in Edmonton and I was in Toronto, we talked about meeting somewhere in the middle. The Canadian Heartland. Saskatchewan, perhaps. Saskatoon. I liked that idea. I'd never really been out there before, in the prairies. It would certainly offer a solitude that would serve us well on our mission. Eventually this idea morphed into situating ourselves on the western edge of the province of Alberta, just minutes away from British Columbia and smack dab in the middle of the Canadian Rockies. A chalet in the deep woods of Banff would be the location.

Having never been in that part of Canada before, I used the typical online tools to conduct some research before booking our accommodations. I was relatively flexible, but I at least wanted the walls to come together to physically touch and form actual corners in a place I'd be sleeping in. I'd stayed in some pretty rustic cottages in the past, and in the past is where those places need to stay.

I saw some pretty daunting stuff in my internet search. Despite the fact that one of the places in Banff I was looking at was billed as a four-star hotel, some woman was screaming bloody murder about it online. In support of her ranting, she had posted an actual photo of what looked like two pieces of white rice. Her claim was that these were in fact bedbug larvae. *Jesus.* Whether her claims were accurate or not, I moved on to the next option. The World Wide Web can be such a blessed and cursed thing at the same time.

Eventually, after having invested my trust in the photos and comments of complete strangers from the internet, I settled on a place called Castle Mountain Chalets between Banff and Lake Louise. I resolved myself to the fact that these things will always be educated-guess crap shoots, and that it's almost better when you don't have assuage from the interwebs leading your thinking. My impressionability doesn't need any further encouragement.

With the accommodations and my flight now confirmed, it was time to focus on the music. My head was swimming with the ridiculous potential this excursion held as I dialed Garvey's phone number.

"Hello, friend," Garvey greeted, in the same tone with which Seinfeld greeted Newman.

"We're booked, man. Flight and chalet sorted. I'll send you the itinerary shortly."

Shortly is a word I like to use when I don't have a specific timeline in mind to complete a task. Somehow it sounds much more efficient than 'soon', even though both words represent the exact same intention.

"Fuckin' A," Garvey shouted.

"I'm stoked, brother. Hey, how many guitars have you got there?" I asked.

"I've got a twelve string and a six-string. I was contemplating renting or borrowing a second six-string, but that would be a luxury and not a requirement. In any case, no need for you to travel with one," Garvey assured.

"That's much appreciated. Kind of a pain in the ass to travel with a guitar."

"No sweat. I've got the sound dock for the music covered too."

"Okay, great," I responded.

Throughout the evolution of this process, the sky had been the limit - we had initially considered bringing vinyl and a record player to augment the stripped-down, natural vibe of this adventure. Eventually, practicality triumphed over substance. I like my iPod in the same way I like Las Vegas in comparison to say, Nashville. There's a terrific economy in efficiency that can't be denied, but the iPod's digital coldness lacks the genuine soul of the vinyl format. Practicality would force one big iPod playlist, but the process of pulling out records from their sleeves, putting them on the player and lowering needle to groove to experience that warmth would have been the preferred medium, by a long shot.

"Are we still looking at doing whole albums, or do we want to focus on songs?" Garvey asked.

This was a very good point. Earlier on we had considered albums as the focus, with key songs selected from those albums as representations of their esteem. But what about those specific songs that do it for you where the rest of the record leaves you cold? Streamlining would be required.

"You know what? You're right. I think we have to do songs in lieu of albums. We can always talk about the importance of the overall record, but we can just take the songs from it we think best convey that importance."

Already, this thing was starting before it actually started. The exchanges were being mentally conjured as we shaped it. The juices were flowing already, and we still had several weeks before go time.

"You realize how vast this is going to be, right?" Garvey asked. "I've got stuff that takes me back to my childhood, songs from the 50s that Mom used to listen to. Special stuff. Chicken soup stuff."

"That music makes you feel something special, right?" I asked.

"Oh yes," Garvey immediately responded.

"Then it has to be included. That's our entire objective here. Bring it *all*."

I hate lists.

One of my imperatives was that I wanted to avoid any shuttered formalities a list may impose. One of these formalities was a numerical limit - top 50, 100 best, 200 greatest of all time - you know. All that crap. There were no limits here, and there would be no rankings or order of any kind. We would bring anything and everything that elicited that special feeling that made our skin vibrate. It just had to be special. Realistically speaking, and knowing us, I figured these guidelines would yield somewhere between eighty and one hundred and thirty songs each.

"I've been free associating a long goddamn list. It's a fun little mindfuck exercise. My criterion is Feel, with a capital F," Garvey told me.

"Good. All part of the fun. And Feel is what we're going for with this," I responded. We were both pretty excited about the whole endeavour at this point.

"I might do my playlist today," I added.

After I heard myself say that, I knew it would actually take much longer than a day. The compilation of these songs would be a significant undertaking.

"My list will be under construction until I'm forced to stop. This has ceased to be a simple collection. It's evolved into a long mix tape of songs that make me feel something. I don't know if we'll get through this in two or three days, but every song I bring in will be worthy of discussion," Garvey continued. "I'm assuming that we'll be listening to all of these songs and not just talking about them?"

"We have to," I replied. "That's important."

"Okay. So - one rule. With recognition that we don't want any rules, of course. Every song identified must be listened to in its entirety, just like in The Record Game. We can't cut a song short just because we've both

5

heard it a thousand times, or because one of us doesn't like it. We have to respect and consider any tune identified as inducing some sort of genuine feeling. Right?" Garvey stipulated.

Whoa.

The Record Game.

My mind went back in time for a moment when he mentioned it.

When we were younger, Garvey used to host parties that were centred on his massive, milk-crated vinyl collection. Music didn't just play in the background at his parties, nor did girls commandeer the stereo to play parts of songs they wanted to dance to. Music was a dependant variable at Garvey's parties, which I believe is how The Record Game came into being.

The game was played like this: everyone at the party had a turn, and when it was your turn, you ran your finger across one of the many milk crates containing the records without looking. When your finger stopped, you pulled out the record your finger landed on. One whole song from that record had to play from start to finish, no matter what the record was. The selector of the record got to pick the song. It was either reward or punishment for your selection. If it was Kris Kristofferson, so it was. You sucked it up. At the end of the song, the record would be removed from the turntable but could not be placed back in the milk crate, in order to avoid potential repetition. The result would typically see the record get tossed across the room, depending almost entirely on the popularity of the selection. Putting the record back in its sleeve was optional, meaning it rarely happened after the first five or six Molson Goldens were consumed. The Record Game was a time-honoured tradition at Garvey's place.

"Yes, I absolutely agree," I responded to Garvey. "There has to be an established level of respect. There can't be any judgment. I'm actually going to try to hear new things that I maybe hadn't heard before as I listen."

"We can bring advertising jingles to the table if we please. No limitations."

"Hey, whatever blows wind up your skirt, man. Nothing is off limits," I confirmed.

"Know what else, motherfucker?" Garvey sang through the phone.

"What else?"

"You might hear some Jay-Z."

I knew he was screwing with me. There would be new learnings and likely some surprises, but I knew Garv wasn't a hip-hop fan. Least of all a fan of Jay-Z. He was winding me up based on my acute dislike for Jay-Z's preposterously self-aggrandizing lyrical bullshit.

"Yeah, because he makes a Yankees cap more famous than a Yankee can. Christ. He should be kicked in the goddamn nuts for saying that, by the lineup of actual Yankee players and real New Yorkers who would no doubt be willing. I'd line up. I'd be happy to kick that guy in the pills," I replied.

"Jay-Z cares very little that you want to kick him in the pills," Garvey intoned.

"That makes me want to kick him even harder," I responded.

A pause. Then Garvey's continued mockery.

"That makes him care even less."

I laughed. "Fuck you. Get to work on that playlist. I gotta get going."

"Alright," Garvey said. "I'm not going to think about *why* until we're in the bunker."

I considered what would comprise my own list for a second after he said that. I didn't know if I could avoid thinking about *why* for that long. Hell, thinking about *why* is virtually all I do in my life.

"Really excited about this," Garvey added before hanging up. "Whatever 'this' is."

CHAPTER 2

Can't Find My Way Home

I sat on the carpet of my music room, admiring the banks of compact discs spanning from floor to ceiling. They carried a certain warmth; a venerability an old friend might have. I was anticipative, and as my eyes moved over the collective, I wondered where the hell I would start.

My greatest concern was making sure I didn't leave anything out. I had to include every song that needed to be included. I didn't want to miss anything. This meant scouring my iPod for any songs that weren't present in this CD library. And further to that, I also had to consider any songs that I may not have anywhere in my overall music collection that made me feel something. There had to be a handful of these to be evaluated. Would that swirling, descending pipe organ riff in Freddy Cannon's 1962 hit single "Palisades Park" still induce the same feelings of excitement in me that they did when I was a kid listening to the songs my mother held dear as a teenager? Upon listening to it again after all these years, turns out it did. But only…*kinda*. Really, it only traced the obvious nostalgic connectivity to my life as a carefree child. And a lot of music did that. I'd be here for a bloody year compiling all of those songs. These days, "Palisades Park" really just made me wonder if Aldo Nova scammed that organ riff for his biggest hit, "Fantasy".

I was looking for the stuff that generated a genuine visceral, physiological reaction in me. Songs that had that groove and made me (believe I could) dance. Songs that choked me up and left me feeling a bit wounded. Songs that made me feel like I could instantly condense a Toyota Corolla into a soda pop can with my bare hands. Songs that lifted me off the ground with their power. *Those* songs.

I could really like a song, maybe even *love* a song, but unless it tweaked that area inside me that other people may call a soul, I couldn't include it here in good conscience. I realized quickly that it would be the songs that felt like they *should* mean something special to me - but didn't - that were particularly difficult to deal with.

Take Billy Joel's *Turnstiles* album, for example. It's a special record, right down to the cover design. Album art of the 70s and 80s sought to paint a picture that encapsulated the songs from the record into a singular idea that the listener could, and should, consider as they listened to the music. The front and back cover were always directly linked by some 'before and after' happenstance.

The Rolling Stones really kicked this concept off in 1969 with *Let It Bleed*. The front cover of *Let It Bleed* featured the record itself being played by an old phonograph arm, but with a peculiar sculpture stacked above it in the place of other records, created from a tape canister, what looks to be a pizza, the dial of a clock, a bicycle tire, and a cake with icing including little figurines to represent the band members. The back cover shows the sculpture in tatters - the record smashed to shards, a piece missing from the cake, the tire slashed. Powerful imagery, from an album whose name was likely meant to be a subtle jab at The Beatles' *Let It Be*. These images spoke with corollary that added greater dimension to the overall offering, however we cared to interpret them.

Billy Joel's albums thrived on this concept back then. Joel's cover art was right up there at the vanguard of this movement, ahead of Styx, ahead of Supertramp. With Joel's 1980 release *Glass Houses* for instance, the front cover shows a leather and denim-clad Joel poised in front of a large glass-walled edifice with rock in hand, cocked back and ready to smash the place up. The back cover illustrates the result - Joel standing in a reticent pose, now wearing a tie, a broken pane of glass between him and the observer. The *Turnstiles* album deploys the exact same format. In it, a despondent-looking Joel is crammed in a subway turnstile among a collection of his urban brethren - an old woman, a young nonplussed child, a glamourous couple, an affluent businessman, and other societal representations. Then - *presto!* The back cover shows only Joel, left completely alone and even more despondent, leaning on a turnstile in the now completely vacant subway station. These visual portrayals might be considered breezy hyperbole even more intensely today, but for me the passing of time has honoured them with a certain charm. I miss that stuff, because it contributed to the overall experience of the album.

And yet even still, as much as I like *Turnstiles*, the record didn't quite trigger that special feeling in me - that physical sensation that courses through the body like an electric current. "New York State of Mind" is on this record, a song I consider to have the most potential for emotional occupancy of all of Joel's catalogue, much more so than "She's Got A Way", "She's Always A Woman", and any of his other songs about romantic love. But none of this music instills any kind of special feeling in me. I really enjoy and even revere these songs for their artistic worth, but I just feel like they don't belong to me somehow. They're not for me. This doesn't discount their obvious quality, of course. They're just not mine.

I have to be honest with myself about the application that Joel's music and all other music has in my life if I'm going to do this right. I'm setting the bar pretty high here. So in compiling the collection of songs that make me feel something, I have to also acknowledge the potential for negatives - the stuff that I do really like but that doesn't specifically move me, and how that could be considered stigmatic.

Even though it's not at all my intention to commoditize music in any way, the smooth jazz stylings of Sting's "Dream of the Blue Turtles" make it immediately identifiable as a chill-out record for me. And chilling out doesn't make me feel anything other than mellow. It's kind of emotionless for me. It wouldn't be attributable to any special emotion or resultant sensation I would actually be inspired to *feel*. As such, "Dream of the Blue Turtles" could thus be considered an emotionless record, even though it's obviously not.

I'm overthinking this already.

And Journey. They're an interesting consideration. Their greatest hits CD sits here on the shelf, having not been played for some time. Every one of these songs aches to be added to my feel collection, the disc literally being a powder keg of emotional TNT for the average listener. Not for me though. Journey's emotionality always seemed to border on being artificial to me. It seemed overt and overwrought. I didn't want to feel it, as much as Steve Perry's raspy vibrato sought to envelop me in its melancholic charms.

I was particularly non-interested in *feeling* Journey. But there were other songs and albums I felt like maybe I should feel. Paul McCartney's second post-Beatles record *Ram* was a great example. I thought this only because McCartney was responsible for more than one of the songs that really did make me feel a special way. One of those songs was from The Beatles' *White Album*, a gloriously ramshackle, sprawling mess of a record (it's technically called *The Beatles* but more commonly referred to as *The White Album*, and thus referred to as such here).

Ram and *The White Album* share certain similarities. They both have that same unpolished *screw yourself if you don't like it* quality - *The White Album* because it was the sound of The Beatles breaking up, and *Ram* because of the immense expectations weighed upon McCartney's shoulders to release a Beatles-calibre record without John Lennon. *Ram* is a fantastic record, even though critics shortsightedly hated it. And yet despite the fact that I play it over and over again from start to finish and thoroughly enjoy it, there aren't any songs on *Ram* that elicit that tingling of the skin for me.

Because I was introduced to *The White Album* when I was twenty and only heard *Ram* many years later, I attribute my greater emotional attachment to *The White Album* to a heightened susceptibility I had to music's power to emotionally engage, given my age and lot in life at the time. Being a twenty year old undergrad in an entirely new social setting, I was a highly impressionable young man having just begun to discover the vestiges of who I may actually be. I was just finding myself at this time in my life, having almost completely washed off the awkward muck of teenage identity confusion. I was embarking on something new, and music played a large associative role. I wasn't looking for answers when I discovered *Ram*, but I was certainly looking for them inside the music of records like *The White Album*, a perfect soundtrack for substance-fueled personal reconfiguration.

And I did find some of those answers back then (for the record, Charlie Manson and I differed somewhat in what we would find). These discoveries are commemorated with significant emotional heft, and the specific songs I gravitated toward can be regarded as tokens of that discovery. And that's where the *feel* comes from. Everything we take from music is rooted in how we receive it through the prism of our own personal experiences. Music will always be modulated by our own individual biography.

And then there are those songs, only maybe three or four of them in all, which just seem to have your number emotionally. You know the ones. We all have them. "Handbags and Glad Rags" is one of mine. This is a big, beautifully written song that ruins me every time I hear it. Yet the lyrics aren't sad at all; they don't really even carry any emotion. The song is about a man telling a young girl that fashion doesn't rank so highly on the list of things that are truly important in life. It's those chord changes that get me. First, the F# minor chord begins the bridge, the familiar harbinger of what's coming next. Then the E chord props me up on the ropes to allow for the subsequent A chord, followed up with a B, to both rip my heart out of my chest. The D chord then holds it up in front of my face, showing it to me sullenly as it takes me into the song's chorus. Every time, man. The vocal melody over top of that chord progression is the beautiful enabler that allows for all of this emotional carnage. If my collection of *feel* songs were a country, this song would be their President.

I have the Stereophonics version of "Handbags and Glad Rags" on CD, but knowing that their version is a cover of a song that was actually written back in the sixties (and not by Rod Stewart, by the way), I look through iTunes in search of any other versions that may be available. Turns out there are more than a hundred of them, from all manner of bands ranging from impressive to embarrassing. I decide to drop what I'm doing for a minute and indulge myself in this fiasco.

Rod the Mod's version of this song is one of the most popular. It isn't bad, but it's a bit flat and the tempo is wrong. This song has to be played slower, with greater intention. Even ol' Englebert Humperdinck throws his hat in the ring here, but his version is predictably milquetoast and gag-inducing. There's a hard rock version of the song here that is completely soulless and devoid of any feeling whatsoever - it reminds me of that unfortunate House of Lords cover version of Blind Faith's "Can't Find My

Way Home". It's still astonishing to me how some people can miss the point by such a ridiculous margin. You just shouldn't fuck around with certain things, y'know? There should be some sort of regulation in place to curtail these ugly misfortunes. There are some really nice renditions here however, notably versions by Jodie Blommaert, Pete Willen, and an outfit called Sunscreen.

Turns out going through all of these permutations of "Handbags and Glad Rags" proved a meaningful exercise, in that I was able to gain a greater appreciation for the instrumentation of the song, and what really needed to be in there. And the piano, the woodwind lines, and the smoky vocals all definitely need to be in there.

But I still had a lot of work to do. Enough with the distractions of iTunes. I could be in there for hours digging through that 'listeners also bought' section.

So after going through my CD collection and gathering up most of the songs that would appear in my playlist, I still had to go through my iPod to source out anything I may not have had on disc.

I prefer to create my own genre classifications on my iPod. The labels of 'Rock', 'Blues', and 'Alternative' are too generic. I don't particularly care for labels in the first place, really. Where do you put Ryan Adams? G-Love and Special Sauce? I've always felt like labels and segmentation are to blame for the path popular music has taken since around the time of the early 60s.

Back in the 60s and 70s, musical slotting didn't exist. Everything was loose and wide open. Mick Jagger could sing with a country twang if he so desired, and Led Zeppelin could release a mostly acoustic record after their first two blistering hard rock efforts. Musical performers were artists, free from genre segmentation. As media began to proliferate, bands aligned with their streamlined models. Rock radio stations had formats that were to be followed, and if bands wanted to get airplay, they had to acquiesce. Print media worked the same way. They employed journalists that bands tried to impress, and those bands lost their way in trying. All this while record companies started to figure out that they could make so much more money selling brand imagery. Bands like The Beatles could write songs that told stories, about anything - a place called Penny Lane, wood that happened to be Norwegian, or the desire to be a paperback writer - because they weren't so tightly bound by their brand images. It seems like today's songs are intended products of the specific brands pushed on us by their performers. Lyrical content is one-dimensionally limited to whatever the performer's brand is looking to sell, be it girl power, heartbreak, sex, thug life, teen angst, the fact that the nerds always win, whatever.

Anyway - if we have to use labels, I'll come up with my own.

My labels are more focused on feel (surprise!). For example, Joni Mitchell. For me, Mitchell's music sounds best on a Saturday morning. Sunshine, fresh cup of coffee. Clears the cobwebs. Right? So I would classify Joni Mitchell and similar music as 'Saturday Morning' instead of 'Folk' or 'Soft Rock' (gag). Because there are different types of pre-established musical genres that I also may be interested in listening to on Saturday morning, like say, country, alt-country, jazz, or soul, I would also categorize these as 'Saturday Morning'. I use other such segmentations too, but you get the point.

More obvious names for groupings are things like '70s'. I also use that one. I haven't been in my '70s' folder for some time, but in my scouring of this iPod for songs that make me feel, I need to look through it as well. Three Dog Night's "Mama Told Me Not To Come" nor Black Oak Arkansas' "Lord Have Mercy On My Soul" would make my collection, but Melanie's "Brand New Key" might. There's actually some pretty interesting stuff in here.

Interesting is a flexible term. I don't remember how it got in here, but "Moonlight Feels Right" by Starbuck is here. And it has a fucking marimba solo, for crissakes. Marimba! That's got to be a trivia question in some part of the universe. Does any other song have a marimba solo in it? As I listen, I try to imagine how this ever could have been considered cool in any way. I picture whoever the singer is as looking exactly like Bob Eubanks with his shirt open to his navel.

Here's another interesting song. "Close To You" by The Carpenters carries with it a melancholy that was there from the beginning, before it could be correlated with Karen Carpenter's death in 1983. This is what I tell myself when I hear it, because despite its seemingly cheery intentions it's a depressing, almost creepy song in my view. This was one of those classic dirges from the 70s that confused my feelings as a child in the same way a lot of songs from the 70s did, a decade that featured more melancholy than even the 90s. This song still screws with me a bit. The instrumentation seems flouncy and light, the lyrics have an innocent, saccharine sheen and the message seems intended to be pleasant, but the overall package conveys a dark, unsettling undercurrent. I've always liked this song, but I like it for a reason converse to the one intended by Burt Bacharach. Or maybe not.

My impression of "Close To You" is sorrowful, because when I listen to the lyrics I had always imagined Karen Carpenter singing the words as a lament to a special someone she wanted to be close to, but could not. It seems lonely in that way because she implies a longing, among the longings of several others she mentions in the song. Along with the rueful hopelessness of the lyrics, the melody may also compel the listener to considering swallowing a gun. It's possible that some of us are more readily led down that path than others, I guess. Again, music is biographically attuned - we all hear what we want to hear in songs, and contrast can be wide.

All these considerations were just more grist for the mill, more justification for this musical summit Garvey and I were about to have. Like we needed any.

Now, one last scan of the iPod for anything else that has to be included. I was pretty certain none of the newer songs I had on here would be included, however. Cage the Elephant's "Take It or Leave It" was marginally interesting to me because of the 60s-inflected chorus that recalls The Animals. I'm ambivalent about the fact that this 60s vibe is reduced to an ironic device in the middle of a modern pop song. Half of me likes the song, the other half is disappointed. It feels like manipulation for ill purposes. Kinda like the way our love for the simple Oreo cookie is capitalized upon to create a Vanilla Oreo version, a chocolate-vanilla version, and twenty-six other hybrids of unnecessary Oreo nonsense. This is not progress. This is greedy, consumptive exploitation.

While continuing this scan of new songs, it occurs to me that I only liked Lana Del Ray's "West Coast" single because I imagined it as a secret love letter to Axl Rose. This song just brings me back to the notion that Axl and Guns N' Roses were the last of the real rock stars, and that there are no real rock stars anymore. There's only trivialized uses of the terminology that douchebags employ to greet each other, and to falsely aggrandize the number of drinks they had the night before. I think about how new rock stars can't come to us from anywhere anymore, because there's nowhere for them to really come from. The last real rock and roll game changer was Nirvana, and that was more than twenty years ago. Music likely doesn't mean as much to kids anymore, because they have so many other modes of entertainment with which to occupy themselves these days. That, or it just means something different to them. Music isn't as communal as it once was. Technology has wiped that concept away by providing us with too many touchstones, and isolation is the result.

The prognosis is unfortunately grim. The other day I came across a website that featured classic album covers by bands who'd had deceased members, and the images of these members had been erased from the covers. The Ramones debut record, formerly featuring all four members standing in front of a brick wall, now simply featured only the wall. Nick Drake's *Bryter Layter* album cover simply showed his shoes, Jeff Buckley's *Grace* cover pictured a lone microphone. My first inclination was to try to see some sort of poignancy in this, but it just felt gross - like a sad, unfunny testament to how tasteless and terrifically horrible people can be behind the anonymity of their keyboards. But this website was also a stark reminder of two things. The first is that there's a marked emptiness left behind by the departed. And the second is that this emptiness will remain.

CHAPTER 3

Cross-Eyed Mary

Garvey and I have a longstanding tradition that started sometime in the 90s when we first began to play guitar together. Whenever we sit down with the guitars, The Rolling Stones' "Dead Flowers" gets broken out pretty much right off the bat. Every time. He showed the chords to me back in 1994, and it's that one song that we always really connected on. So whenever we get together, it's kind of a homecoming.

I was properly introduced to the Stones by Garvey, so it made sense that plenty of stuff from their career quintessence - *Beggars Banquet*, *Let it Bleed*, *Sticky Fingers*, and *Exile on Main Street* - got jammed on with the acoustics. I found an old Maxell cassette the other day that had *Fred Garvin & the Salt Peter Players* written on its liner. It was one of the tapes we had used to capture impromptu basement jams from back in the 90s. We would just press record and let the tape roll, hoping that we could capture some of that magic we thought may have emanated from us during the hours after three in the morning, nestled in amongst the ambient clinking of vodka bottles and drunken hooting in the background. There's lots of stuff on this particular tape. "Dead Flowers" is of course included, along with some Neil Young, Eagles, and Blind Faith. Amusing to listen to and think back on now.

These jams were the primal musical expressions of two young, enterprising musical enthusiasts - abandoning songs half way through in favour of others, laughing at missed chords, and generally just revelling in the idea that being able to play our favourite songs brought us that much closer to being inside them. The jams could only be entertaining to the two of us, at first by simple bias and now maybe through nostalgic wistfulness. One song that would sometimes come up in these sessions, started but never once finished, was "Loving Cup" from *Exile on Main Street*. It was one of my favourite all-time Stones tunes. I had never really taken the time to properly learn how to play the whole thing; the beginning was a straightforward D-C-G chord progression, easy enough to play. But the breakdown deployed other more unique chords that I would have had to really listen to a few times to figure out. And that horn part at the end of the song made things even more complicated from an acoustic guitar perspective.

But no matter. For this upcoming meeting, I decided I was going to learn "Loving Cup" from start to finish. I would teach Garvey the parts he may not know. We would still have a little bit of enterprise in us after all these years.

I had resigned myself to the fact that I would never be completely satisfied with any playlist created for this intended purpose. I had toiled through this task for days and days, and still it felt unfinished. Like I was missing something. Or that I had included songs that maybe shouldn't have been included. It's kinda like painting or writing books, I guess - in labours of self-expression, the work can never really be complete. Changes can always be made, tweaks applied here and there. I know now that in the latter stages changes are mostly unnecessary, made if not only to appease the ego.

I'm certain Garvey had felt the same way about the construction of his playlist. My final tally contained just under one hundred songs, after I stripped away an additional eight songs that I convinced myself didn't pass the litmus test. Garvey had told me his song total was in that same ballpark, not quite a hundred. I knew he would still be tweaking until my plane landed in Edmonton. We agreed that there would be no rounding up for the sake of having an even, clean number. This would sully the integrity of the exercise. What you have is what you have, and that's it. I wanted this to be as simple as possible.

It was at once compelling and mildly terrifying to amass this mosaic of music that would define the person that I thought I was. Because really, that's what this playlist is. Honesty played a large role in this project. It would be easy for me to create an artificial playlist by fashioning some broad assemblage of songs that commanded music appreciation cred to make myself seem 'deep'. Obviously, that would be stupid. This was going to be warts and all, man. Naked and vulnerable.

Garvey and I also agreed that there would be no judgment. That was important. There would inevitably be some lighthearted jabbing, but no harsh judgment. And knowing each other as we did, it wasn't like there would be any massive surprises. Would there?

Of course there would be. There had to be. We had almost two hundred songs here. There had to be some unexpected weirdness. That would be part of the intrigue.

I wasn't worried about Garvey's judgment of my playlist so much as I was my own consideration of what the playlist *meant* - these were the songs that represented my development as a person. Music is everything to me, and this playlist would reflect my musical DNA. I was apprehensive about what it could mean. But I was always apprehensive of what everything meant. I always overthink things way too much. My playlist was what it was. Period.

I was interested in seeing Garvey's song collection. Our upbringings were completely different and despite having lived in the same general area, our cultures were entirely dissimilar. Almost to the point where it was unlikely that we would even be friends, in fact. How we were raised clearly played a significant role in the individual shaping of our personalities. But for both of us, music would also factor in considerably. Despite our differences, we both leaned on music pretty heavily growing up. We're very different people on the outside, and yet inside we're very much the same. Music is the strongest tie binding our friendship. This is where my initial interest in this entire endeavour was centred.

Garvey and I both realize our mutual dependency on music far beyond genre, and much of my interest was in the examination of that dependency. Through looking at our affection for these songs, we'd learn a lot more about each other on much deeper levels. And of course, we'd also learn more about ourselves.

BRENT JENSEN

Being sandwiched between a large man and an even larger woman on the four-hour flight from Toronto to Edmonton was not at all appealing to me. I set the personal TV screen positioned in the seat in front of me to that channel that charts the plane's progress over the course of the flight. This channel is a schematic representation that illustrates your airplane making its way across a map of Canada's provinces on course to its destination, with all of the exhilaration you might expect from Pong. But it is useful, in that it's nice to know how far along you are in your flight. It can be somewhat masochistic through the Ontario and Manitoba portions of the trip, but when the little white plane floats across the border of Saskatchewan, things start looking up.

I wasn't going to do this, but I decided to listen to my playlist during the flight. The songs had been placed in the playlist, which I had unambitiously named 'Feel', by dragging them across from the general contents of my iPod. It appeared not to be in any particular order, but it actually was in the alphabetical order of the artist. Except for one small detail.

I created the Feel playlist from a pre-established playlist already in my iPod called Twenty Songs. These twenty songs were put there several years ago, interestingly enough, after Garvey and I had a conversation about songs that would be most important to us if we had to each pick only twenty of them. I had put mine in this playlist so I could burn them onto a CD to send to him in the mail. I had completely forgotten about having done this all those years ago.

So, because the songs from the Twenty Songs playlist were also in my Feel grouping (except two that I ditched), they would now comprise the first eighteen positions of my Feel playlist. Everything else was added to it in artist alpha order. I wondered if Garvey had remembered that we did this. I wasn't sure if I had ever received a CD from him. It was interesting that we'd been working towards this objective all along.

As the screen in front of me refreshed itself and our little white airplane representation steadily progressed forward, I worked my way through my songs. I was intrigued by how crisp and fresh a metal song sounded after listening to a 70s piano ballad, and vice versa. The essence of every song seemed to be renewed when heard in this format, exploding out of the headphones. Listening to songs in this way isn't something I would have ever normally done, just because it would seem so weird and jarring to me, but it really gave them expanded life. I was getting pretty amped up to get past the dress rehearsal and on with the real thing now. Listening to this playlist just made me want the little white plane to move across the provinces that much more quickly.

By the time the plane did finally arrive at its destination, I had been able to listen to the first forty-one songs from my playlist. A small part of me felt like I should have listened to all of them at least once before getting here, to have been more prepared. But prepared for what? I suppose I just wanted to ensure that I verbally represented this music with the substance I felt it deserved. I was concerned about that. But I had to trust in the fact that these things would take care of themselves. This would be a celebration of the music we held most dear. I had to trust my heart to do the talking, and I had to be confident that it wouldn't fail.

Garvey greeted me at the Edmonton International Airport as he always had over the years. Big hug, knowing smile. And as always, highly anticipative of the promise of what always would come during these visits - deep musical appreciation, inspired acoustic guitar jams, and the consumption of our combined weight in alcohol. Life was frozen in place during these visits.

"How was the flight?" Garvey asked.

"As good as it could be in the close quarters of individuals who eschew deodorant," I replied. My nostrils had been treated to that dreaded pungent tang of body odour more than once, compliments of a gentleman sitting directly behind me. Everyone in his proximity knew who it was. He got cut-eye from all of us.

"That's always nice on a four-hour flight."

"There ought to be a law, frère," I replied.

Garvey and I called each other *frère* from time to time. I don't know where it came from, but it likely had something to do with our northern Ontario upbringing.

We made our way through the throng of travellers and towards the parking lot outside. Important sunshine flooded the afternoon here in Edmonton, and I remarked at how surprisingly warm it was for mid-September. We threw my bag into the trunk of Garvey's vehicle and we were away.

"Alright, so - I was thinking afternoon beers and guitars out on the deck, some barbecue for dinner, and then an electric jam tonight with my drummer Ryan at our rehearsal space," Garvey offered.

"All perfect. Love it."

Garvey was always a great host. He had rented a Gibson J45 acoustic from his local music shop for me to play during my stay this time around.

During the short drive back to his place, we caught up on the typical stuff - families, work, current events. Newer stories involving mutual friends we had. Those things. Before long, we would be positioned between his patio deck and the sun with acoustics in our laps and drinks in our hands, ready to identify. When we did arrive at his home, he gestured to a box on the floor containing several bottles of wine.

"We'll bring that tomorrow. What do you think - wine, scotch, and some beer to fill in the gaps?"

"I like that," I nodded.

I was still getting acquainted to the subtleties that separated whiskey from scotch, and both of those from bourbon. I didn't care so much in these situations. My love affair with booze continues.

"I have a bottle of scotch downstairs that we can bring, so we'll just need to pick up the beer tomorrow morning on our way out of town," Garvey suggested.

"Beautiful."

"Hey, do you know what I found yesterday while I was moving some things around in the garage?" Garvey asked.

"A unicorn," I replied.

Garvey's frown implied his distaste for my brand of levity.

"No. Not a unicorn. I found a disc from a long time ago containing songs I had gathered after a conversation we'd had. We had talked about putting together twenty songs that we absolutely loved. The disc had fallen behind some stuff in there before I could send it, and I forgot all about it. We've been working towards this idea even back then," Garv noted.

Hah. Indeed we had.

The sun began its downward descent, first receding behind a neighbour's house before disappearing altogether beneath the horizon. After a few beers and some more chat, Garvey leaned forward and looked down at the deck planks, formed a D chord on the neck of his Taylor with his left hand, and strummed the opening bars of "Dead Flowers". As we always did when playing this song, he sang the verses and I jumped in with him on the choruses. As we played, I mulled my quiet satisfaction in the idea that we still vaguely fancied ourselves as some wayward Mick & Keith combination after all these years.

Our individual vocal approaches diverged in the same way our soon-to-be-revealed playlists likely would - Garvey's singing style had a more rootsy, almost country-based feel to it, while mine had always had that gritty rock and roll inflection I had been anointed with by my musical heroes. Now on the eve of our trip, this song that we had sang together so many times over the decades, would serve as an even more apt metaphor for the complicated edification of our musical brotherhood.

After dinner we were off across town to the industrial area where Garvey's rehearsal space was located, preceded by a quick stop for a few drinks at Garvey's local.

"So just a heads up for you. This place we're headed to is pretty sketch. Don't make eye contact with any of the individuals you see hanging out there," Garvey advised.

I sensed that he was only half-joking. The last time he had provided such an advisory to me was in Memphis in 1998. I didn't take it seriously, and was subsequently almost run over by a tricked-out late model Dodge Shadow. This time I would heed the advice.

"Some interesting characters hanging around your jam space, are there?" I asked.

"I don't know how interesting they are, but they ain't exactly upstanding pillars of the community."

"I know the type. Remember that Guns N' Roses cover band I used to play in?" I reminded Garvey.

"Um...no. Refresh my memory," Garv said before taking a pull of his beer.

"Yeah, you remember. I was between bands and I had an ad out locally looking for a singing gig in a covers band. I got a response from a nineteen-year-old kid, saying that his band did hard rock stuff that more or less lined up with the material I had done with previous bands. Black Crowes, AC/DC, Bowie, Zeppelin, you know."

"Okay, right," Garvey nodded.

"So we talk, and I don't know he's nineteen yet. We're going back and forth asking each other questions, and he asks how old I am. I tell him I'm thirty-four, which I was at the time," I said. "He tells me that he and the other guys in the band are nineteen."

Garvey grimaced.

"Right? So I tell him thanks anyway, but he insists that I come down and jam with them. They did heavier hard rock stuff - Guns, AC/DC, Metallica, Ozzy, and so on. He tells me they're really good, and that I should check it out. That there would be no harm in it. I politely decline, but he keeps up with the prodding."

"So what happened?"

"I did a little bit of research, and found out the band was actually pretty good. So I caved in and we arranged to jam at their rehearsal space."

"Dude," Garvey admonished.

"Hey, listen. I was fresh from coming off trying to find a guitar player for my last band, and it was *grim*. Everyone embellishes their abilities a bit in these situations. Some people embellish *a lot*. This one guy told us via email that he played lead guitar in a band with regular gigs, and I asked him for a song list. He sends back Van Halen and all kinds of other things that require some pretty serious lead skills."

"Right."

"So I say, '*you can play Van Halen's "Hot For Teacher"?*' and he replies yes. So I want to see this guy, and we arrange for him to come down to the rehearsal space."

"Of course," Garvey said.

"His emails are signed Hooman. Kinda weird. I didn't know if that was his name, or what."

"More Hooman than a Hooman…" Garvey sang.

"Yeah, Rob Zombie would have been welcomed at this point. This guy was the latest in a long line of suspicious characters we tried out. You know what that's like."

"Oh yes," Garvey acknowledged.

"So now we're waiting across the street from our rehearsal space, and we see this lanky-looking nerd wheel up on a crappy old ten-speed bike with a gig bag strapped across his back. I say to my buddy, '*hey, could you imagine if that was Hooman? How funny would that be?*' and we carry on and have a good laugh about it. Well, turns out it *was* him. And he was a fucking terrible guitar player. No Van Halen. At all. He could barely play "Seven Nation Army". It was death," I said.

"Brutal. Okay, so back to the teenagers," Garvey said.

"Right, right. So I show up at this place these young guys play at, and it's called Sumenal Studios, located in this run-down industrial area in east Toronto. It's a shithole. The guitar player comes out to my car, and he looks like Slash with brown hair. I'm not kidding. I could barely see his eyes. I'm mildly afraid."

"What was he like?"

"Actually, very friendly. Really good guy. But I'm still not expecting much from the whole thing. So we go inside this dump and get set up, and he pulls out this beautiful Gibson Les Paul gold top and starts playing through a full Marshall rig. And the guy is *amazing*. Slash, Zakk Wylde, Randy Rhoads, all note for note. Phenomenal player. The rest of the guys were great too. So I joined their band, and we played a couple of gigs around Toronto. After about six months we parted ways. I was moving out of town, but I was probably holding them back anyway," I explained.

"So the jam space - not so good?" Garvey questioned.

"That's the thing. The place was an absolute dump that attracted the same crowd it sounds like yours does. The owner lived in an apartment upstairs, and we used to do rock-paper-scissors after every rehearsal to determine who would have to go up there and pay him."

"Really?"

"It smelled so badly of cat piss and whatever disgusting food he was always eating that it would literally make you gag on your way up the stairs. It was horrible," I responded.

"Jesus."

"Yeah. So this place came complete with its own creepy cast of urchin-like characters that may be similar to the ones at your rehearsal facility. Lots of down-and-outs of all ages just hanging around, looking for trouble to get into. We used to have to lock the door when we played, because these weirdoes would barge in out of their minds wasted on whatever they were on, looking to score drugs, cigarettes, money, whatever."

Garvey raised his eyebrows.

"So anyway, there was this one girl who used to hang around a lot. Always looking for cigarettes, maybe looking for something else. I put her on maybe twenty-five years old, maybe a bit younger."

"Yeah," Garvey intoned.

"When you saw this girl from behind, she looked good. Tall, long blonde hair, really nice body. But when she turned around, you could immediately see that her eyes were crossed."

"Like, askew? Lazy eye?" Garvey asked.

"No, dude. Fully crossed. Like, Cookie Monster fully crossed," I replied.

"Fuck, man."

"Yeah, it was bad. The guys called her Cross-Eyed Mary, after the Jethro Tull song."

"Oh, that's nice. But better than Cookie Monster, I guess," Garvey said.

"I know, it was unfortunate. On top of that, she also had this peculiar slur when she bummed cigarettes that added to the general weirdness of it all."

Garvey shook his head.

"And she was always there, she wouldn't leave us alone. Nobody ever fessed up to it, but I think one of the guys in the band may have had relations with her at some point."

"Are we certain that that guy in the band was not you?" Garvey smirked.

"We are indeed certain, you dirtbag. But if Cross-Eyed Mary is there tonight hanging around your jam space, I can't make any promises," I laughed.

Garvey smiled and downed the contents of his bottle. "This is why we're friends."

Garvey's rehearsal space was Sumenal Studios redux, minus the odour of cat waste and dubious foodstuffs. There was a collection of ne'er-do-wells forming a vaguely menacing scrum in front of the main entrance, shadowy figures in the darkness barely outlined by a distant and thus less than effective street lamp. None of their faces would be revealed to us.

Garvey looked in my direction, his eyes telling me *toldja*.

"All upstanding young folks, I'm certain of it," I said to him.

We walked past the shady gathering and into the building. These places were all the same, no matter what province, state, or republic you were in. Concrete, wood, and stinking worn carpet, barely lit and unevenly smeared with varying shades of black paint. The walls were replete with graffiti scrawled in childlike cursive vehemently urging its audience to defy authority, disrespect everyone, and of course, to fellate its author. Garvey's jam space was a room down the hall that contained much of his and the rest of the band's gear. His band's drummer Ryan was there already, so the door was unlocked.

Taking in the vibe of this little musical emporium made me long for the days of belonging to those gritty gangs that we called bands, the jam space being our hallowed clubhouse - personalized with smug reminders that this was a place of intended ill refute, rough and reckless and unrepentant. It was a place that never failed to take me through an entire range of emotions. It provided calm refuge against the obligations the outside world continually heaped on my shoulders, at the same time sparking the excitement of inserting yourself into the role of singer, guitar player, or whatever else you chose to be. In this place, you experienced that beautiful magic of actually *generating* the beloved music, an exhilarating endgame of childhood bedroom tennis-racket-guitar dreams. I missed the chemistry, the camaraderie of the band proper; I missed that incendiary sensation collectively experienced when all the band members locked in together and touched that third rail in unison. Special times. I smiled wistfully looking around this room.

"Whaddaya wanna play?" Garvey asked, a Fender Telecaster already strapped over this shoulder.

I pulled another Tele from a holder affixed to the carpeted wall behind me and plugged it into one of the amps on the floor.

"How about "Jumpin' Jack Flash"?"

We smashed through the procession on heightened adrenalin, sweaty and possessed. I howled Jagger's lyrics into the mic, a bit hypnotized by the moment. And there it was again. That unforgettable pull. The *fire*.

The three of us ran through some Black Crowes, some Tragically Hip, and a handful of other songs before Ryan had to get going. Garvey and I stuck around for a couple more, for old times' sake. Two old friends getting musically reacquainted and massaging a bond that lay ever susceptible to the strain of time and life's forward progression.

As we played, I thought about how ironic it had been that despite having jammed together so much, and having been in a number of different bands, life had always gotten in the way of us ever being in the same one together. But times like these, at maximum volume inside this fraternal den of iniquity, pushed those considerations aside for a little while. And they would continue to do so in the years to come. I would make sure of it. We had always done well to find brightness in the night.

CHAPTER 4

Crikey!

Just after nine in the morning.
We had three quick stops to complete in Edmonton before heading south through Red Deer to Calgary, with a hard right onto the Trans-Canada Highway that would take us straight into the mountain range that divides Alberta and British Columbia.

My buddy Eckley had told me before I left Toronto for this trip that he had experienced two specific moments in his life that literally did take his breath away. The first was seeing Detroit Red Wings hockey legend Gordie Howe's blood fall to the ice during a scrap with an opposing Toronto Maple Leafs player at centre ice in Maple Leaf Gardens. The second occurred as his family's car turned that corner on TCH1 that allowed him his first glimpse of the majestic Canadian Rockies, rising up from nowhere out of the prairies, monolithic and awe inspiring.

I was certainly looking forward to this same moment, even if my mind was primarily on the music as we scanned the local grocery store shelves for our supplies. I wondered about how this whole caper would go down.

"Bacon good?" Garvey asked.

"I'm not really a bacon guy, but go ahead," I responded.

Garvey dropped the package into our shopping cart.

I don't typically eat bacon. Too greasy. Instead I delude myself by choosing sausage as a healthier substitute.

"Grab a bag of those little potatoes, and I'll go and get some cream for the coffee," Garvey said. "Maybe get some of those bell peppers to grill with the steaks too."

My mind was elsewhere. Would we get through all of the songs? Was it too late to make changes to my playlist? *Dammit.* I couldn't stop thinking about all of these bloody considerations.

"Alright, I think we're good," I advised when he returned, taking one last look at the cart before maneuvering it towards the checkout. We had everything we'd need out there now. After our last stop at Tim Horton's for a couple of large double-doubles, we finally hit Highway 2 South. The blurry digital aquamarine segments in Garvey's dashboard indicated it was eleven o'clock. This meant we would be at the Castle Mountain Chalets just before three in the afternoon. No need for stops along the way, neither of us wanted that. We couldn't get there fast enough.

Highway 2 sliced straight through the centre of the prairies, which were bathed in sunlight and splayed across countless miles in every direction. The sky was cloudless, endless azure. I soaked up all of this scenery from the shotgun position in Garvey's Mitsubishi RVR as we clicked off the kilometres that stood between us and our promised land.

Once he and I worked through the more sobering details involving the present and intended future tenses of our lives, our automobile discussion was then followed by a measure of loose flotsam and jetsam, the nostalgic sort that always emerged as a preferred component of lengthy, isolated road trips. These conversations, rapacious little re-examinations of mutual history, are decidedly mandatory. They're always replete with vaunted star players and psychotic miscreants drawn from the mass of characters encountered along life's long way, malleable now, and often made more amusing by the passing of time than they may have actually been. A round of 'whatever happened to her?' is followed by a recounting of related stories that may or may not have already been shared previously. For the most part they had, but that wasn't important. This recitation was necessary. The information we traded back and forth would do its part to keep their legend legendary, despite what Facebook would have us believe about their current existences - expanded waistlines and lost youth be damned.

"Are you friends with Marley on Facebook?" Garvey asked.

Marley was a mutual friend decades ago back at Laurentian University, a great guy with teen heartthrob looks and Errol Flynn statistics. In his freshman year alone, we estimated he must have covered the entire female contingent of our dorm. At least the portion deemed worth covering, anyway. He was demi-godlike among the rest of us, but he carried an earnest modesty that likely made him that much more attractive to the ladies. Marley had little need for Facebook back then.

"No, I'm not," I responded. "How is he?"

"He's doing well."

"Did he ever take over his dad's construction business?" I asked.

"Not sure. I saw a picture of him and someone else standing in front of a movie theatre. Seems to me he bought it with another guy, and that's what he's doing now."

"Marley had twin daughters back in the 90s," Garv went on.

"Yeah, I had heard that."

"I saw the family pictures on his Facebook page." Garvey turned his gaze away from the road to look at me. We both started laughing.

"Aw Christ," I replied. It stood to reason that Marley had gone on to marry a beautiful female and that their offspring would not be unpleasant at all to look at.

"Poor dude. Karma's a motherfucker," I said.

Before we left Edmonton, I had put the Castle Mountain Chalets information into my iPhone maps app and brought up the route we would take down Highway 2 and across the Trans-Canada Highway. Over the years, I had come to rely on this application completely in lieu of traditional paper map use or the writing down of directions. I even preferred it to GPS. It was just so easy to use. And now, the radiating little blue dot that represented us in the app had bypassed Calgary, headed west toward the mountains of Banff. It looked as though we had about thirty minutes of driving left.

After one last short stretch of flatlands, I finally saw them out there in the distance. Grey pointed obelisks, revealing themselves with more and more detail as we approached. They were incredible to witness. The sheer scale of these mountains was indescribable - it immediately became clear how incredibly small everything and everyone was in their presence. I sat transfixed as we entered the Rockies proper, mesmerized by each new vantage point a bend in the road would offer. Snow caps could eventually be seen on the peaks of the mountains as we continued our approach, along with the detail of the thousands upon thousands of pine trees that dotted the bases of these massive pyramids. Eckley was right. It was indeed breathtaking.

"Dude, this is fantastic," I said to Garvey. He had seen it all several times by this point. He nodded.

"They make you realize just how small you really are, y'know? Like a gnat. On the back of a rat."

"Hah. Did you rhyme that on purpose?" I asked.

"No I did not, as a matter of fact," Garvey replied.

"Yes you did. Eminem has nothing on you, sir."

"Eminem has very little in the first place, frankly."

Garvey turned to look at me, his eyebrows raised and his mouth forming a large smile. "Know what else, pally?" he said excitedly.

"What else?"

"I have a surprise for you."

"Is that right?" I said. "And what would this surprise be?"

Garvey gripped the wheel and grinned with glee. "I got mushrooms for us!"

"Are you fucking kidding me?"

This *was* quite a surprise.

"Nope. Not kidding. I got them from a buddy a few days ago. Wait until you see these things, they're totally different."

My immediate reaction was apprehension. I hadn't done 'shrooms since the early 90s, more than twenty years ago. My mind began to sort through those incidences in an attempt to acclimate. I could only really remember taking them four times, though I'm sure there had been more. My first instinct was always one of caution these days, even if it was unnecessary in this case. I never used to be this way.

"What's different about them?" I questioned.

"They come in pellets now, not those bitter little pieces that used to get stuck in your teeth and stuff."

"Pellets? I gotta see this. Mushrooms. I can't believe it. What if I freak out and start having hallucinations out there in the woods?" This was completely unlikely, I know.

"That won't happen. Come on, think about it. What better place to do mushrooms than out in the mountains?!?!" Garvey exclaimed.

He was clearly stoked about this, and there was no reason I shouldn't have been as well.

"You're right, man. I'm in," I said. "Been awhile, that's all."

"It would be weird if I took them and you didn't," Garvey said.

"Yeah, that might be a bit strange."

"They just make you laugh. No big deal."

Indeed they did. The first mushroom recollection that came to mind was the night I was visiting a friend at his parents' house, back in school during the Christmas holidays. His parents were away, and we drank in his basement with plans to go out to a bar later that night. We took the mushrooms on a lark at the last minute. A short time later, I became fascinated with a pair of his dad's reading glasses. They were these funky old-school orange-rimmed numbers, so uncool that they would likely be considered ironically cool now by anyone who had a beard and wore skinny jeans, a natty sweater, and a stupid hat. In my delirium, I thought it would be funny to take these glasses into the bathroom and look at myself in the mirror. I remained standing in front of the bathroom mirror for more than an hour, staring at myself wearing the glasses and laughing my ass off.

Now, the more I thought about this, the more I was interested in rediscovering the power of the magic mushroom. All the memories were coming back.

"I took 'shrooms with Myles one night," I said to Garvey.

Myles was a senior who lived with Garvey in dorm at Laurentian. He was a grand ringleader of chaos in the eyes of all who knew him. Everybody had a Myles story. One that got told a lot was the time when Garvey hosted a party at his parents' house when they were away for the weekend, and Myles jumped into the pool wearing Garvey's mom's fur coat.

Garv looked back at me with a grin. "How did that go?"

"Pretty much as you'd imagine. I remember seeing him sitting in the back of a pickup truck by himself outside the party we were at, so I climbed in to chat him up a bit. After I stepped over the tailgate he looked at me with big eyes, and his face just kinda froze in this expression of dread and fear. He kept mumbling '*Jesus, Jesus*' and didn't move. He looked astonished."

"Myles always looked astonished," Garvey said.

"This was a bit different. I upped the ante a bit by standing there with my legs crossed and I raised my arms mimicking the crucifixion, and then he really lost it. I was laughing like a hyena. He explained to me later that my head happened to be directly in front of a street lamp from his perspective, and my hair was longer then, so all he could see was a silhouette with this bright halo behind my head and he had this freaky Jesus hallucination. We sat down together in the truck after he got past the Jesus thing and marveled at a tree about fifty feet from us that seemed to be growing Rubik's Cubes rather than leaves."

"See? How could you not want to take these things?" Garvey lamented.

"You're right. Silly me," I responded. I can be illogically paranoid sometimes.

I looked down at my iPhone to see how close we were to Canmore, which was where we had decided to stop for gas. The glowing blue dot appeared on the left side of Canmore. Meaning we passed it.

"Fuck, we passed Canmore," I blurted out.

Garvey looked in the rearview mirror.

"Shit. What does the phone say, how far are we from the chalet?"

It looked like we were about ten minutes away. I expanded the screen with my thumb and forefinger. Uh-oh. Maybe longer.

We took an off-ramp a few kilometres down the road that appeared to lead to a gas station and a McDonald's, but we found neither.

Back on the highway.

"We might be able to make it to the chalet on this tank. It's gonna be close. Banff should only be a few minutes away. Is Castle Mountain Chalets right in Banff?" Garvey asked.

"Yeah, it looks like it based on this. Have a look," I replied.

The red pin, representing the address of our destination as provided on the Castle Mountain Chalets website, looked to be just off of the main downtown street of Banff.

"I know where that is. That's great. I've been in this area of Banff before. If we're staying there, we're right in the middle of the action," Garvey said.

My understanding was that we would be located out in the woods, but I could have been wrong.

We eventually arrived in Banff and proceeded into the downtown area to gas up the vehicle. My body vibrated faintly as I stretched outside and took a deep breath of fresh, clean mountain air. The grandeur of this place was not lost on me.

We got back into the vehicle and drove to the spot where Castle Mountain Chalets was situated according to my phone. But it wasn't there. This was strange. We must have missed it somehow.

We circled the area a few times looking for the road named in its address, each time growing more tense, but it wasn't there either. This didn't make any sense.

Eventually, Garvey pulled into a parking lot and called the chalet's number via Bluetooth. A woman answered.

"Hello, Castle Mountain Chalets, Jessica speaking." Her accent sounded British until it sounded Australian.

"Jessica, can you tell me why my iPhone is telling me that I'm at your chalet, when I'm clearly in a parking lot with no sign of a chalet anywhere to be seen?" Garvey seethed. He was not happy.

"Oh dear. We're having a real problem with that, I'm afraid. Google provides customers with the post office box where we receive our mail as a destination, rather than our actual address," Jessica fretted over the speaker.

Garvey shook his head in disbelief.

"Are you kidding me? Good lord."

"I'm terribly sorry about that, sir. We really need to get that sorted, and we're working on it. But can I give you directions from where you currently are?" Jessica offered.

"Yes please," Garvey exhaled icily.

A number of female Australian faces ran through my mind as Jessica's voice provided instructions detailing how we would find her. I settled on Kylie Minogue. Nicole Kidman was a close second.

We got back on the highway, headed in the opposite direction now. Jessica's instructions took us back to an area we had driven by fifteen minutes ago, marked by a sign that read Castle Mountain.

Garvey and I looked at each other. "Now, it didn't say *chalet* anywhere on there, and Google's dependability level up to this point has been pretty strong for me," I rationalized.

"Does the fact that we're specifically literal human beings work to our advantage or our disadvantage?" Garvey wondered aloud. I didn't have a particularly profound answer for him. We both just wanted to get there now.

After a few minutes of driving, Garv posed another question that would prove difficult to answer.

"Do you think that Aussie girls scream out '*crikey!*' when they orgasm?"

"Of course they do," I replied.

"Jessica sounds young. Do you think she's hot?"

"I'm going to say yes. I feel like it would be unusual if she wasn't hot."

Garvey looked away from the road to frown at me.

"I'm putting this in the book. You know that, right?" I said.

"Well, I want you to do what you think is right, young man," Garvey drawled in the stupid, exaggerated old man voice we both often used to mock each other and ourselves. That voice would be used several times over the next few days.

And now, to our left, the previously fabled Castle Mountain Chalets at last appeared. We had finally reached our destination. We pulled into the parking area in front of the main office. We were taxed by a lengthened drive, but emboldened by the promise this excursion held. We went inside to check in.

"You found us finally!" Jessica welcomed us in an Aussie brogue that was even more pronounced in person. Her fresh-faced good looks neutralized any previous Google-related tensions. She was likely an undergrad, or newly post-undergrad jacking it up for one last summer - delaying the inevitable by taking the time to get a handle on her life direction before making that point-of-no-return leap into the rigours of adulthood. We've all done it. Some of us are still doing it.

"So you guys have the one-bedroom chalet right?" Jessica asked.

Silence for a moment. Then Garvey responded.

"Yes," he muttered under his breath. We looked at each other with immature expressions the way Jack Tripper and his buddy Larry from upstairs may have in this situation. There was a pullout sofa in the living area. Practicality had trumped bravado.

"Okay, you're all set," Kylie Minogue concluded. "Do you have any questions for me?" Garvey smiled a wry smile at her.

"No. Not yet, Jessica."

"Alright then. Enjoy your stay with us," she smiled back.

CHAPTER 5

Two Minutes to Maestro

There we were, at the centre of the incredible majesty this great country has to offer, faced with the task of determining what in fact is so bloody important about music.

I wondered what answers would come.

Our living accommodations over the next few days would be more than comfortable. Simple and rustic. But a clean, modern, rodent-free rustic. The kind you want when you come out here. The walls of our chalet bore the natural beauty of real timber, and its A-frame structure raised the ceiling to make it seem much bigger than it looked online. It had a full kitchen, a massive bathroom complete with shower and Jacuzzi, with a second door leading to a bedroom with a king bed topped with a crisp white duvet that couldn't possibly be host to bedbugs. Three skylights lent additional brightness to that already provided by several windows. The large sitting area just off the kitchen had a sofa with two chairs, and a stone-faced fireplace stocked with firewood, kindling, and the previous day's newspaper. These implements would all be replenished daily by Jessica and her post-undergrad selfie-taking peers.

"You want the bed, Garvey?" I asked. I didn't care.

"No, no, no. You've travelled a long way to get here, pal. I don't mind sleeping on this," he said as he pulled out the bed from the sofa and left it exposed. "Let's make sure Jessica and her friends see that it's actually being used."

But it had likely been too late. Conclusions had probably already been drawn regarding the two strange males who were not from around here, renting the chalet with one bedroom. Castle Mountain may as well have been Brokeback Mountain.

What was left of the afternoon had ebbed by the time we loaded everything into the chalet and got settled. We sat in pressure-treated Muskoka chairs on either side of a small wooden table on the front porch of our cabin, Castle Mountain's grandeur positioned directly in front of us. I waited for the sense of calm to come. Garvey set up the sound dock on the table and opened his first beer, having already consulted the pillowcase of weed he had brought along with him. I promptly followed suit with a beer of my own.

"Cheers," I said, clinking my bottle against his.

"Well?" I asked. "Shall we begin?"

I was ready to finally get into this, and yet not without feeling a mild trepidation at the same time. I didn't know exactly what to expect. I didn't know what failure would look like in this endeavour, or if it was even possible. But I was considerate of it nonetheless. I guess I just wanted to open myself up to this as much as I possibly could, without holding anything back.

Garvey was not wary whatsoever. He was blissful, in fact.

"Alright. So how do you want to work this?" he questioned. "It probably makes more sense to go one-for-one rather than to let one playlist go on for a bunch of songs, no?"

We hadn't talked about any of this. No planning had actually been discussed in terms of how we would carry this out, but going back and forth song by song was definitely the best approach.

"Yep. One-for-one is the way to go," I replied.

"We don't want for one of us to tune out and lose interest while the other plays song after song after song," Garvey said.

"I'm not worried about that. You're going to be completely riveted by each and every song on this playlist," I said as I held my iPod up to his face. This, of course, was a completely inaccurate statement.

"That's highly unlikely, but we can go with whatever format you want. This is your show."

"Hmmm," I paused. "What if we develop a seething hatred for each other before this is over?" I wondered aloud.

"Now *that's* likely."

Smug response. I expected nothing less.

These were considerations I had actually made during the weeks leading up to this moment. There wasn't any danger of coming away from this thing *hating* each other; that was impossible. It would be unreasonable to even consider something like that, since we had been like brothers for so many years. But - what if this exercise compelled us to think lesser of the other? We agreed that there would be no overt judgment in a pragmatic sense, but what if our playlists precipitated some sort of silent perception of flaw, of weakness, significant enough to permanently alter our kinship in a negative way? Theoretically the possibility absolutely existed; but we would have had to be pretty goddamn shallow to even entertain it after everything that we'd shared over the years. It wouldn't happen. Couldn't.

Regardless, at this moment of putting it all out on the table, it occurred to me just how brave this was. We were all the way out here, alone in the middle of nowhere for several days, surrendering our most basic feelings to each other in detailing why we adored the music that we did. The emotional exposure stakes were pretty much as high as they could be. Our relationship would have to be altered in one way or another as a result.

"There will be no judgment, frère," I said, and I did mean it.

I already had a vague idea of what would comprise the majority of his playlist after knowing him for so long. And what I didn't know I looked forward to learning about. These songs were the sinews of what my friend was made of, and I wanted to see things from the inside. Regardless of what it might look like.

"Yes, I agree," Garvey responded. "There can be no judgment."

"There can and will be subtle mockery, but no judgment," I confirmed.

I knew we would wind each other up at many points. We always did.

"Alright, who's going first?" Garvey asked.

We both looked at each other in a periodic stalemate.

"You go ahead," he said and sat back in his chair.

I looked at him with a smile and inserted my iPod into the dock to set up the first song on my playlist. Keith Richards' snarling open G guitar riff announced my first selection, "Can't You Hear Me Knocking", from The Stones' *Sticky Fingers* record. I felt a jolt of adrenalin course through my spine. Garvey smiled that familiar smile of approval.

"Oh yeah, man. It's on my list too. Very nice start," he nodded as that crisp Charlie Watts snare kicked in, soon joined by Jagger's sneering vocal. This was perfect rock and roll.

"That raw, dirty groove is wholly representative of everything that The Rolling Stones should be remembered for," I said.

I wanted to say that this was my favourite Stones song, but doing so would be a grim prospect. There were so many others, if even just on the *Sticky Fingers* record alone.

We sat speechless in our Muskoka chairs, quieted by our awe in this recording. I looked up to the snow-covered peaks of Castle Mountain opposite our porch as the song morphed into an extended Santana-flavoured jam, led by guitarist Mick Taylor's solo.

The calm had come now. This was bliss, finally.

"This is an authentic spur-of-the-moment jam. Apparently Taylor just kept playing, not knowing that the tape was still rolling. Some of the other guys put down their instruments, but as Taylor kept playing they picked them up again and jumped back in," I told Garvey, even though he likely knew this already. But I loved those obscure little facts that lent even greater meaning to how songs like this one made me feel. Our time here would no doubt be a musical geekfest flooded with these exchanges of information.

"Your turn, man," I said after the song had ended. I pressed pause on the iPod to prevent my next selection from playing and removed it from the dock.

"We'll have to be careful of that as the night progresses," Garvey warned. "I could see us just letting the iPod run, forgetting what we were doing in our delirium."

"Nah, I think we'll be alright," I replied.

And I did. I was too compelled by this. Not only to hear Garvey's songs, but also to have him hear mine.

He locked in his first song, "The Great Pretender" by The Platters.

We had talked about this over the phone. This song had been a barometer that tested the boundaries of our song selection, right before we agreed that absolutely nothing was off limits.

"This is my aural chicken soup," Garvey said wistfully. "It provides me with a lot of comfort. It conjures up that warm feeling of watching my mom enjoy it so much, swaying slowly back and forth while it played. Very meaningful. It's Mom Music for me."

"Perfect. Because that's what this endeavour is all about," I said after downing the warmish, unpalatable remainder of my beer.

I didn't know what was next on my iPod, nor did I want to know. That was part of the fun. After Garvey paused his playlist and removed his iPod, I inserted mine and pressed play. That opening piano line, as it always had been, was even more stoically beautiful out here in this setting. My next song was Sir Paul McCartney's "Maybe I'm Amazed", from his first post-Beatles solo record before Wings would be formed. I looked over at Garvey. He smiled and nodded in the affirmative. Even if we didn't want this to be about approval, it would be virtually unavoidable.

"I was lucky enough to see Macca live a few years ago," I started. "Instead of just running through the songs, he set this very intimate tone by talking a bit about the numbers he would play before he played them. Despite the fact that there were seventeen thousand of us on hand in the arena, it almost felt as though we were guests in his home. Like he was just casually playing songs for us very informally. The guy is just a master class entertainer. The entire show was so great, but for me there were two specific highlights. The first came when Paul sat unaccompanied on a stool and played "Blackbird" on an old beat up acoustic, telling a story beforehand of how he used to write songs with John in the parlour of John's parents' house before The Beatles took over the world. He didn't phrase it that way, of course. But "Blackbird" apparently came from fooling around on their instruments the way they did back then. The second highlight came when Paul went behind the piano and dedicated the next song to Linda, and launched into "Maybe I'm Amazed", again unaccompanied by the band. Very emotional," I told Garvey. "I'll never forget it."

Only a few songs in and already I could feel the power of what we were doing.

Garvey's turn now. His next song was "Only You", by Yaz.

I hadn't heard this song before. I did recall former Yaz member and contralto-voiced Alison Moyet's big single "Invisible" making the rounds on MuchMusic in favour of other videos I'd have preferred to watch back then. I had also heard of the album this song came from, *Upstairs at Eric's*, but I had been preoccupied with the devil's music at that time. This was new territory for me.

"When Dad was coaching the women's basketball team at Laurentian, he often listened to the same music the players were listening to. I remember going on recruiting trips with him and listening to *Upstairs at Eric's* over and over again in the car. Alison Moyet's androgynous vibrato and the electronic music combined to sound delicate. Pretty. I like that she comes a little unhinged at the crescendo. Desperate sounding," Garvey said as he stared at the wooden planks forming the floor of our porch.

"Well done. I like it," I said.

Garvey looked up, breaking his meditation as the song ended. He took a drink from his beer.

"You're up."

I looked at my next song before inserting the iPod.

Whoa.

Big, thick slabs of distorted guitar, pounding drums and thundering bass all blasted out of the sound dock at us at the same time. I felt strangely redeemed for some reason. Motley Crue's "Looks That Kill" crashed the proceedings.

"This song is just fucking incredible," I expressed with a massive grin. I couldn't say anything else. Articulation seemed unnecessary. I wanted to let go of words altogether and just howl in approval of something that made me feel so expressive. This music was just primal savagery. Garvey looked on in bemusement, like a father watching his son ride a roller coaster for the second time.

"I saw the ad for *Shout at the Devil* in Creem magazine in 1983, ran out and bought the record, and I had a new musical super-infatuation. It was like boarding a rocket ship into another world. Motley Crue was everything I was looking for as a fourteen year old kid in a stimulus-deprived small town. And "Looks That Kill" was my anthem. I literally felt electrified the first time I heard it, like I had been struck by lightning. Simple riff, four-on-the-floor drums, and yet so big and so compelling - almost tribal in feel. That's the attraction. That tribal-ness of it."

I was increasingly thrilled by the promise of what we were doing now. Screw trepidation.

After a while the empties began to limit space on our table. I opened up a bottle of wine in preparation for takeoff. I didn't know when it would come, but the countdown was already on.

Garvey accessed his pillowcase and pressed play on his next tune, Richie Havens' "Freedom".

"I love this song, man," Garvey said. "I have these early memories of watching Woodstock with my Uncle Barry, and through all of the performances, including Hendrix, I was struck by this one in particular. The intensity. The tribal rhythms. A busted string. *All* feel."

Yes. I could hear it. That feel. This wasn't quite my cup of tea, but I understood what I was hearing. I understood what it meant, what Havens had intended to convey above the woozy din of what was Woodstock. I savoured what I felt as we sat there, the two of us breaking musical bread in this holiest of places. It felt like I had hoped it would.

I was up, and Ryan Adams' "Goodnight, Hollywood Boulevard" was next on my playlist. Realistically, this song was one of a number of suitable representatives from the unvarnished musical collection that was Adams' 2001 record *Gold*. It was one of my all-time favourite albums, versatile and heartfelt almost in an ugly way. There was a reason I chose this particular track to represent the record, however.

"Do you remember the story behind this album?" I asked Garvey as Adams' thick, spare piano chords filled the Alberta air.

"Umm…story?"

"Yeah. It was Christmas break in 2001 I think, and you were home from school for the holidays. I was up in Sudbury visiting family and I dropped by your house for drinks one night. You were in the basement listening to music, and when I came down the stairs "Goodnight, Hollywood Boulevard" was playing. After listening to it for a bit I asked what it was, and you said it was a new album that Tony from Records on Wheels had recommended to you."

"Ah right, right," Garvey responded. "I had asked him to set me up with something, and he suggested this record to me. Tony's recommendations were always money."

"And as we listened to the rest of the record, you said that you figured I would like it too, and so you went back to the store to pick up another copy knowing I would be over at some point. But Tony had sold you the last one," I continued.

"Yeah, I don't remember exactly how that went," Garvey said.

"Ah. Maybe you just made that last part up back then," I suggested.

"That's entirely possible. But it *is* the thought that counts, after all."

I smirked as I took a drink from my wine glass.

"Your turn, jackass."

"Okay, this next song represents the entire album it comes from as well," Garvey said as his iPod made a *ka-chik* sound as it fit into the dock. I recognized the grey weariness that emerged after he pressed play.

"Is this "Highway Patrolman"?" I asked. The album was Springsteen's *Nebraska*.

"No, "State Trooper"," Garvey responded.

I had picked up *Nebraska* along with most of the remainder of The Boss' back catalogue recently in anticipation of the album's stripped-down solemnity. But I could only listen to it a couple of times because it was actually *too* solemn, too punishing for me. Too much like a depressing cloudy afternoon. *Nebraska* succeeded in delivering exactly what it proposed - the album cover features a colourless, dreary grey sky, a visual equivalent of the gloom of the record. I related my perspective.

"I respect the integrity of this record, but I can't listen to it. It's like the soundtrack for Camp Kill Yourself," I said.

"Is that a thing?"

"No. But if it was, *Nebraska* would be the soundtrack."

"The whole record is bleak. You can argue that you don't like *how* it makes you feel, but you can't say it doesn't provoke a feeling," Garvey said.

"Absolutely agree with you," I replied. "I don't deny its power. I wish I *could* listen to it. I like the story behind it."

"What's that?"

"That Springsteen recorded the demos in his bedroom at home on a four-track, brought the songs in for the E Street guys to record, but then shelved the band recordings in favour of the mood and feel of his demos. Springsteen wanted to release the demos as they were, to retain that feel. And the record company wouldn't release the record at first. Not until he promised them an upbeat, fully electric album immediately after, which turned out to be *Born to Run*."

"Nah. *Born to Run* came out before *Nebraska*," Garvey corrected.

I paused. "Oh, sorry. Right. I meant *Born in the USA*."

I could thank the wine for that little bit of overenthusiasm. Even still, Garvey was the Springsteen expert. He had pored over *Nebraska* and the entirety of the Springsteen canon for years, and knew them with intimacy. I had always been intrigued by this notion, regardless of whether or not I was willing to admit it at first - peering over the fence to see what was going on cerebrally in his musical backyard, beyond what was happening in my own. I had always been keeping an eye on the shade of his grass, I suppose. And now, out here, I was *in* his yard, smack dab in the middle of the lawn as it was growing around me. If its scale made me feel small, then it was an even more thrilling juxtaposition between my own musical egocentrism and my enthusiasm for what I perceived as growth.

My next selection, The Carpenters' "Close to You", had made me feel enough to warrant its inclusion in this exercise.

"This song was definitely on my radar," Garvey admitted from his chair on our porch, as two young staff members walked by and smiled meekly.

"Don't mind us," Garv continued as they passed. "We're just two men sipping wine and listening to 70s soft rock in solitude."

I laughed an unconsciously hearty laugh. I could thank the wine for that too.

"The 70s screwed me up as a kid," I said.

"What do you mean?" Garvey asked.

"There just seemed to be a lot of duplicity in media. Songs with bouncy, florid instrumentation carried these disparaging lyrical undertones. It sounded like Karen Carpenter was smiling when she sang the lines of

"Rainy Days and Mondays", and it unsettled me as a young kid. I paid a lot of attention to these songs because the radio was always on in our house when I was growing up, and I spent a lot of time listening to it by myself. Really keying into it. Music was my most accessible stimulus, and because it felt so connective I probably transposed my own emotive framework onto songs I heard the most. I guess I went ahead and felt what I imagined the songs were asking me to feel. But oftentimes the messages seemed confusing and a bit twisted to me."

Garvey snickered.

"And television shows used the same weird, thinly-veiled menace by casting otherwise likeable personalities like Wayne Newton and Paul Williams as murdering villains, wearing those mysterious black leather gloves and strangling women to the creepy glissando piano score playing in the background," I continued.

Now Garvey was fully laughing and nodding. "No man, you're right. I don't disagree."

"Right?" I started laughing myself. "The goddamn 70s corrupted me!"

After our laughing fit had subsided, it was time for Garvey's next song. As it began, I recognized neither the song nor the singer.

"Who's this?" I asked.

"It's Meat Loaf. This is a song called "For Crying Out Loud"".

It had always intrigued me that an obese man chose to go by the stage name of Meat Loaf and expected to be taken seriously. And it intrigued me even more that he actually *was*. But then again, the 70s…

Garvey continued. "Again, I would just select this one song as a representation of the whole record. My earliest explorations through my parents' record collection were driven by the cover art more than the music. *Bat out of Hell* was the best possible album cover. And the record was theatrical, operatic, and dramatic. The music vacillates between making you want to cry and drive your car really fast."

"Can't argue that. I was always gripped by that bizarre exchange between Meat Loaf and…what do his friends call him? Meat?" I asked.

"I think his real name is Martin, so probably that."

"Yeah, I guess. Anyway - the exchange with whoever the female vocalist is in "Paradise by the Dashboard Light" - wherein Meat, or Martin, is trying to get her to do the deed in his car but she's resisting because she questions Meat's commitment to her. And then that weird sports broadcaster comes in during the breakdown, calling the carnal play-by-play using the old around-the-bases metaphor. Who the hell would have ever thought that would be a good idea to put into a song?" I asked.

"Turns out it was," Garvey replied.

"The dashboard light tune was popular with a girl I was mixed up with once. The sexual subject matter of the song was the source of a peculiar fascination. Music was always there to lead me by the hand through all of my social learning experiences as a teenager, and whether I like it or not, songs like that one serve as pretty powerful totems of my youth. And y'know, in this way, highly intimate soundtracks for our lives were created for us by circumstance rather than by our own choosing. We didn't have a choice," I said.

"Don't get too philosophical yet. This is only my fifth song," Garvey said.

"It's true though, do you know what I'm saying?" I persisted. "Meat Loaf's "Paradise by the Dashboard Light" carries a mild stigma for me because I link it to an unfavourable memory."

"Unfavourable? I thought you said the song's sexual innuendoes represented a fascination?"

"I also said the fascination was unusual."

"I think the word you actually used was *peculiar*."

"Either way, it ain't always good," I said.

"Unless of course you're into German porn," Garvey pointed out.

"Let's move along then. Now brace yourself for my next song," I warned after looking down at my iPod. It was "Two Minutes to Midnight" from the all-powerful Iron Maiden. I beamed with pride as I pressed play and the opening riff ripped through the sound dock.

Garvey smiled knowingly. "I was wondering when this was coming," he said.

"This song would be on a very short list of songs that defined my adolescence, Garv. It's fundamental metal from a band that isn't really a fundamental heavy metal band, and that's what makes it truly great," I postulated.

"Right," Garvey acknowledged. He was encouraging my enthusiasm, even if heavy metal interested him very little.

Before long my favourite part of "Two Minutes To Midnight" was approaching, that gorgeous section where the breakdown ramps back up into the main riff to slingshot the song forward like a locomotive.

"Listen to this - right here…" I continued with a child's anticipation just before crunching power chords signaled the moment. "The drum fills are so precise, played with an almost jazzy swing-style feel, that they add extra excitement to the transition to really elevate the song."

As the crescendo came, I raised my hands in unison like a conductor as if helping to lift the music up and fill this place with its power. I was completely into it. That familiar tingling sensation rose up through my skin, the sensation I embraced like a junkie.

"Maestro!" Garvey cracked.

"Conduct like there's nobody watching," I responded.

When the rush subsided I flashed a massive, vulnerable smile to Garvey, sat back in my chair and took a drink from my glass.

"Good lord," I croaked.

"You could use a cigarette," Garvey observed.

My smile remained. There was no better place to be.

CHAPTER SIX

The Needle and the Damage Done

Garvey took a lengthy pull from his peace pipe. Our surroundings were quiet enough that I could hear the crackle of whatever was burning in there.

As we sat on the porch together awaiting the nighttime, Garvey prepared his next offering. We presented these songs to each other as if they were badges that announced our authority to speak on a subject that had granted us enough enlightenment to do so. We were sincere in hoping that our words would work the way we wanted them to, doing adequate justice to what the music stirred inside us. But we wouldn't ever be completely assured of this. I wouldn't anyway. The music had always felt too big for that.

A vibrating harmonic *ping* came out of the sound dock. Then another, higher in tone. The two notes continued their back and forth volley, the immediately recognizable introduction of Buffalo Springfield's "For What It's Worth". I nodded in appreciation.

"All you need are those two ping-ponging notes. The bass, guitars, and everything else are just gravy. It's intensity without bluster. Genius stuff, man," Garvey said.

As we hashed through the genealogy that included Buffalo Springfield, Crosby, Stills & Nash (and sometimes Young), The Hollies, and The Byrds, the song came to an end and Garvey's next song began to play.

"Fuck. Sorry," Garvey disparaged as he reached over to hit pause. I didn't recognize the song.

"No worries. What is it?"

"It's "49 Bye Byes", Stephen Stills from the CSNY *Four Way Street* record."

"Stephen Stills?" I said. "May as well leave it on. Retain the flow."

"Alright, sure," Garvey said, reaching for his glass instead.

"Unless there's a pre-arranged order in your playlist, I suspect your next selection is also from this record," I suggested with a smile.

"It is," Garvey confirmed.

"Let's let it roll then," I responded.

The next song would be Neil Young's solo acoustic medley from this live album, comprised of three songs - "The Loner", "Cinnamon Girl", and "Down by the River". I guessed this correctly only because Garvey had himself gotten me into this years ago, knowing I was a Neil Young fan. I used to listen to it over and over again back then. In my mind, this medley was ground zero classic Acoustic Neil - grit, conviction, and fragility. It could have easily been in my playlist.

"Even though it's only Neil playing one guitar, it sounds like more than one doesn't it?" Garvey asked as the medley began.

"Oh yeah," I responded.

My favourite thing about Neil Young from back then was that jagged edge that emerged in both his guitar playing and his singing. He played acoustic with a fluid, rhythmic groove with little concern for proper technique or perfectly clean notes. His voice was higher then, and he sang with a fairly impressive vibrato that followed the same rationale - a cracked note every now and again lent it character and legitimacy.

"I always wondered why he chose to go to "Down by the River" after "Cinnamon Girl" in this medley. The transition doesn't really work as smoothly as the first one did, from "Loner" to "Cinnamon Girl"," I said.

Garvey shrugged his shoulders, not looking away from the sound dock. "What do you think would have worked better there?"

"Um…you could go from the G, or the D that starts the verses. So "Sugar Mountain" or "The Needle and the Damage Done" maybe," I answered.

"Tempo wouldn't work," Garvey said, still fixated on Neil's playing.

We used to form our own Neil Young medleys during acoustic jams by connecting common chords from his songs. I used to go to "Ohio" from "Southern Man" and to "Sugar Mountain" from "Old Man" and then on to whatever else came to mind if it worked. I'd make a game of it, sitting around by myself just to see how many Neil Young songs could be fused together. But listening to Neil now made me consider never playing another one of his songs again, just out of sheer respect for the man's passion.

Garvey exhaled and leaned back in his chair as the song ended, shifting his attention to me. "This album was my earliest foray into listening to music with headphones, just lying in bed as a kid and listening in the dark. It added so much more dimension and range. And this was my introduction to Neil Young, this incredible acoustic medley," he said.

"Very cool. Y'know, I never really did use headphones very much but I wish I had. I didn't like the idea that the headphones limited me from hearing anything else. As a young kid I was listening to KISS with headphones once and my mother had been calling me to the phone from another room. She eventually came up behind me and grabbed my shoulder, and I had to be scraped off the ceiling. It scared the crap out of me. Never really used the cans after that."

Garvey snickered. "You dork. It's your turn."

"Finally," I sniffed as I retrieved my iPod.

One of my absolute favourite records would be represented next - Van Halen's *Women and Children First*. I may have had a couple of representative tracks from this album on my list, and now I was about to foist "Take Your Whiskey Home" onto poor Garvey fairly early in the game. He was very much a non-believer in Brother Edward and his band.

"Who's this?" Garvey asked when confronted with the snappy strains of an acoustic guitar that sounded nothing like Neil Young. I knew as soon as I told him he would be repulsed.

"These are the guitar stylings of the mighty Edward Van, my friend," I announced.

Garvey smirked and nodded his head in recognition. Better reaction than I had expected.

"I love the sloppy swagger of this record. Van Halen is a band with exceptional amounts of musical talent, and here they're making a record that sounds loose and gloriously raw, but never on purpose. All the bum notes and background noises are kept in, because that's what makes this music real. It's not slick, and it has guts. It's an attitude record," I continued. I could have gone on and on all night about this album.

"There will be no judgment," Garvey replied politely with a smile.

"I get that bluster of this sort is certainly not for everyone," I assured, making reference to the divide in our musical tastes. I liked that the division was there at moments like this.

Having had an appropriate amount of drinks, I could have gone on a full-out *Women and Children First* jag after hearing that track. But that wasn't what we were here for. Well, not really anyway. Garvey *ka-chiked* into the sound dock to cue up his next musical exhibit.

The song began with the crowd noise of a live recording, clear enough to indicate a seemingly smaller venue, and what sounded like a woman conducting some sort of chaotic, hyper-enthusiastic beatnik poetry reading. Whatever this was, it wasn't familiar to me. As the band came in behind the female poet, she transitioned from slam poetry into the first verse as the song began to take flight. The vibe implied that wretched artfulness of The Ramones, and I imagined the setting of this recording to be New York's CBGB. What I heard next jolted me out of my chair somewhat. The last word in the last line of this verse startled me, forcing my eyebrows up higher than Justin Beiber's.

"Dude, what the fuck is this?" I asked, looking at our surroundings from left to right. We were still outside on the porch, and the music was likely louder than it should have been.

"This is "Rock and Roll Nigger" by Patti Smith," Garvey answered, effusing the same level of pride Ricardo Montalban did as he welcomed his guests to *Fantasy Island*.

I cringed. For me, there remained only three words in the English language that still carried enough potency to truly shock, and the n-bomb was one of them. I had certainly never heard this song previously. Didn't even know it existed. I understood the context of the message Smith was conveying, however. It was loosely related to the context Elvis Costello used when he described *one more widow* and *one less white nigger* in his single "Oliver's Army".

"Jesus, man. You're going to get us kicked outta here with this stuff," I joked as Patti Smith kept right on screaming the word into her mic, over and over again, reducing Johnny Lydon to something less remarkable.

"This is a perfect rock and roll song. This was rap before rap was rap, with crazy freestyle slam poetry, and backed by the world's tightest punk band," Garvey glowed. He was loving the abandon.

"What year did this come out?" I wondered.

"1978, I believe."

"When was Blondie's "Rapture" released, around 1980?"

"Sounds about right, yeah," Garvey responded.

"So Smith was technically 'first' in that case."

"To rap, you mean?"

"Yeah. I was just thinking about Blondie's "Rapture" video, with Fab Five Freddy in that white suit wearing those glasses that lit up, remember? The fact that she rapped the whole coda of that song almost made it seem like two songs in one at that time. I didn't quite appreciate the gravity of what she was trying to do in leveraging hip-hop as a white female punk artist back then, but the freakiness of it did get my attention. It didn't seem terribly out of the ordinary, but it would prove to be progressive later on."

"And Patti Smith?" Garvey questioned.

"That definitely got my attention. And I'm sure the effect was that much more blistering in 1978," I replied.

"You're up, frère," Garvey noted as he got up to fill his glass. "Whaddaya got for me?"

"I have a song that harnesses a different type of power. This song never fails to choke me up every time I hear it. Iron & Wine's "Each Coming Night"."

Ka-chik.

Garvey's head slowly nodded along to the picked acoustic guitar notes as they flowed out of the sound dock.

"Iron & Wine?" Garvey pronounced.

"Yeah. It's a guy named Sam Beam, who uses the stage and recording name Iron & Wine. The same way Dan Bejar does with Destroyer."

Garvey tilted his head back and then down in one long motion without looking at me to acknowledge this information, seemingly intent on the song.

"I like this," he expressed.

Towards its end, the song slowed itself for its final verse; that gorgeously doomed bit that consistently breaks me. I braced for impact, even though I really wanted for the song to ruin me. I always wanted that, regardless of any other intention I seemed to have had.

Sure enough, the song fulfilled its bleak promise once again, pulling me into its vortex for that one fleeting but intense piece of time to demonstrate its power. Then it let me go, leaving me to consider the impact of that moment as I always would do when it ended. It's astonishing how some songs can so easily manipulate your emotions in this way. Astonishing and gratifying. And even more so on this day. Everything was so much more intensified out here.

Neither of us spoke when the song concluded. I raised my eyebrows at Garvey. He knew.

I inhaled. "You're up."

Counting Crows' "A Long December" was Garvey's next song. The Crows had been masters of melancholy long before this song came out. Garvey and I had played *August and Everything After* countless times during the summer we spent together in working at a marina on the north channel of Georgian Bay.

"So many Counting Crows tunes to choose from," Garvey explained. "This isn't my favourite song of theirs but the imagery is vivid. It's got that one line - *the smell of hospitals in winter* - it's just thematically perfect. The timing for this song coincided with a period of my life when I smelled a lot of hospitals."

I nodded in silence, partly in recognition of the mild pall that had settled over our heads. It was that time of the day, and the music nor the wine were helping. We listened together quietly as Adam Duritz's sentimental vocal coloured outside the lines.

I contemplated my opinion of Duritz as I listened, which tended to lean toward the negative for reasons I hadn't really thought about at any great length. Maybe it was his shabby dreads and his generally glib predisposition. It could have been the Tasmanian Devil-like swath he cut through two-thirds of the female contingent of the *Friends* cast, along with a number of other A-list Hollywood hotties. Maybe it was the petulance he demonstrated in not playing Counting Crows megahit "Mr. Jones" during their live shows at the height of its popularity. Perhaps it was all of these things, and maybe a few others. Dude was certainly talented though. I had to give him that.

"I really should have included "Around Here" in my playlist," I lamented. "Duritz does something special with the lyrical melody lines towards the end of that song. You know what I mean, right? The *'she's always on my mind'* part?"

Part of me wanted to reach for my iPod and play the song at that very instant, until I realized how much I sounded like that obnoxious girl at the party pretending she's drunker than she is, insisting on taking over the sound system so that she can play "All About That Bass".

"Yeah, I know what you mean," Garvey responded. "Duritz has this incredible knack for singing in and out of the bars, the same way Van Morrison did. Not just staying confined to the song's measure. He has a great sense of timing."

Just then an overpowering roar came out of nowhere, jolting us somewhat. Ah, right: I had read about this while having a look at Castle Mountain Chalets' customer reviews.

The train.

The handful of chalets here were very close to a railroad line that seemed to almost cut through the property in a location where it crossed the main road. There were no gates or barriers, so approaching trains had to sound their horns constantly as they passed through. On Castle Mountain Chalets' website, an embittered overnight guest claimed that trains passed through at a rate of two trains per hour. That seemed a bit excessive to me. But people always exaggerate shit like that when they're angry and want to make a point. We'd already been here for four or five hours, and this train had been the first we'd heard. And trust me, it wasn't like we may have just not heard any previous ones.

"You care about that?" I asked Garvey, motioning with my chin towards the train as it snaked away.

"Nope," he replied. "It's not like it's going to keep us awake at night."

Garvey was right. The booze would see to it that sleep, whenever it did come, would be deep.

The gentle, hushed swing of Led Zeppelin's "Down by the Seaside" came next. I listen to this quite a lot, mostly via full plays of *Physical Graffiti* or through another playlist I had created entitled 'Sunlight'. This song connected me with relaxing thoughts of being outdoors, in valuable sunshine on mellow summer days.

Garvey smiled when he recognized it. "Nice."

"This is one of those songs I equate with summertime. I listen to it mostly when it's sunny outside," I told him. "I do the same with Joni Mitchell. In fact, I don't listen to Joni Mitchell at night. At all."

He started laughing. "What? Why?"

"For the same reasons I don't listen to Van Halen or AC/DC in the morning. It just doesn't work," I resolved.

Garvey shook his head. "And this is a rule, is it?"

"Yes, it is, as a matter of fact."

I knew this was unusual, but it was true and I felt strongly about it. I suppose I could listen to Joni Mitchell in the evening if I really had to for some reason. But never AC/DC in the morning though. That just wouldn't be right.

"We should think about eating something soon," Garvey said above Jimmy Page's tremoloed guitar. Across the footpath directly in front of our chalet was an open gazebo maybe seventy-five feet away, housing a large stainless steel barbecue that looked to be in much better shape than I would have expected.

"Sure. Let's hear a few more songs and then we can get started on dinner," I said. I went into the chalet to get another bottle of wine and a bag of chips as "Down by the Seaside" approached its conclusion.

"My next song's going on whether you're out here or not," Garvey shouted with equal parts sarcasm and melodrama.

I laughed. "I'm coming, you fucker. Hang on!"

These were the best times. Loose, easy times.

I returned to my chair with a fresh bottle, dropping a bag of Ruffles on the already crowded table. "Roll it."

The distinctive drum riff immediately made me smile in appreciation. U2's "Bullet the Blue Sky" was Garvey's next number.

What we were doing here took on a bit of a *This Is Your Life* flavour - the anticipation of which potential old friend would come through the door next, followed by the joy and excitement that followed when you were reunited.

"Roaring, dive bombing, buzzsaw guitar. Ominous, lumbering bass. Impending fucking doom. Bono channels a Baptist preacher during one of his now patented mid-song rants. This song feels like ducking for cover to me," Garvey deliberated.

Even further to the perpetual *This Is Your Life* thrill, I took added pleasure in experiencing songs I already knew quite well in a completely different light, through the eyes of someone whose musical tastes I respected. It had never occurred to me before that The Edge's guitar on this track was 'doomy' sounding - I had always been too consumed with Larry Mullen Jr's drum riff, the way he made the hi-hat hiss in between the unorthodoxy of his snare drum thwacking. But yes, the guitar feedback is harnessed effectively, and those little nuances The Edge contributes throughout does lend an apocalyptic feel to the song. I had never really paid attention to that before. It almost felt as though I was hearing this song for the first time again almost thirty years later. It made me want to listen to the whole *Joshua Tree* record over again. I was pretty sure I also had a track from this record on my playlist, I just didn't know when it would materialize. Maybe next, maybe a couple of days from now. I made a point of not looking at my playlist until I had to. I didn't want to know what was next.

When I eventually did have to look at my iPod, I saw that my next tune was "The Needle and The Damage Done" by Neil Young. This was a brilliant, heartfelt song. The first note elicited an instant smile from Garvey. We let the beauty of the spare acoustic passage wash over us for a minute.

"When I first became familiar with this song at school, another guy from dorm and I listened to it at least twenty times in a row. Despite the fact that it's only Neil and his acoustic, it feels like there's so much more going on in there," I said.

"Were you stoned?" Garvey asked.

"No, I wasn't. I was just fascinated. I hadn't really heard anything like it before. The other guy had, but he was content to just keep rewinding and rewinding. He might have been stoned. He was stoned a lot, actually," I recalled.

I continued with the memory.

"The song was on one of those little 'cassingles'. Remember those? It was 1989 and I had just returned to school for my second year, after having bought this really badass Nakamichi cassette deck from a guy I had worked with at the paper mill over summer vacation. Dude was about five years older than me and had all kinds of high quality audio gear. He was that guy in town who always had the nicest, most expensive stereo. Anyway, CDs were just really gaining popularity in the mainstream at this point, and I still had loads of cassettes so I figured, why not? He was more or less handing it off. We both had a lot of walkaround quid from the mill. Student employees at the mill got *paid*, man."

Garvey nodded.

"So, now I'm building my first real stereo. I have this Nak deck, a Yamaha receiver I traded for a bunch of student meal plan cards with someone in dorm, and two massive speakers I traded with someone else for a twelve-string acoustic guitar. After it was finally assembled, the first song that would play through that Frankenstereo was "The Needle and The Damage Done". It was exactly two minutes in length, and as soon as the applause came in at the end of the song and that 2:00 showed up on the display, we would just keep hitting rewind without really paying attention to how many times we had rewound it previously. Had to be at least twenty times. Growing up a metal kid, I had never really paid attention to a song like that before, and I just couldn't get enough of it. It sounded so honest and desperate to me. It just flooded me with feeling. Really opened my eyes. Not only was this song my introduction to the brilliance of Neil Young, it also marked the official beginning of my foray into bands like The Beatles, The Stones, Zeppelin, and everyone else I had stupidly overlooked in high school."

"Classic rock, you mean?" Garvey asked.

"Yeah, but there's something about the term 'classic rock' I don't like. It reminds me of those radio stations that bleed this market by running songs like "You Shook Me All Night Long" into the ground. I feel like the term 'classic rock' homogenizes the musicians who tend to fall under that categorization, y'know?" I responded.

"Is there a better term?"

"I just try not to use one at all."

Garvey smirked at me. "Should we rewind "The Needle and The Damage Done" one more time, considering you talked over the whole thing?"

"Play your next song, you fucking joker," I responded.

CHAPTER 7

Welcome To The Jungleland

"Ah. Interesting," Garvey noted as he looked at his next selection. "This is my Springsteen gateway. The first song I heard from the very first Springsteen record I ever had. "Jungleland". It's practically a radio program through which you listen as desperate young Turks strive for significance on the Jersey shore."

Garvey had always had a much deeper breadth of sociopolitical awareness than I did, and I wondered if Bruce Springsteen hadn't helped him out with that somewhat. During our teenage years, while I was listening to tales of girls with large chests and cat-like features being deflowered in elevators as told by their Aqua Netted hair rock paramours, Garvey was listening to a much different kind of rock. He focused his attentions on epic compositions that soared and plummeted, ones that featured storylines of hope in desperation that culminated in the tragedy of personal despair. In other words, vintage Springsteen.

When Garvey and I first met in 1986 at a week-long basketball camp in Sudbury, we were chalk and cheese. I was a mulleted smartass who mouthed off first and asked questions later. Garvey chose to sit back a bit further, being more comfortable in his own skin. We were cordial with each other, but by no means did we strike up any kind of a friendship. Not even close, in fact. Social demarcations were razor sharp back then. You either *were*, or you *weren't*. It was black or white. The only greys that existed were those that coloured the emissions pouring from the factory smokestacks of Sudbury.

Northern Ontario social culture was pretty cut and dried, and you played to your strengths wherever you figured you fit in. I tried my best to blur the lines, to exist in more than one of these social compartments, but I was really a rocker at my core. And Garvey was not. Not a rocker like I was, anyway. We mutually recognized this reality and continued on beyond each other, he in his white *Born in the USA* tour t-shirt and I in my black *Master of Puppets* tee.

We would come face-to-face again in 1990, when our friend groups overlapped at Laurentian University. There was still no connection, even if I had progressed away from my skinny niche label and skinnier black Levis. We had likely still remembered how we felt giving each other those sidelong glances a few years earlier, the same way Arnold Schwarzenegger and Axl Rose did as they crossed paths at the end of the Guns N' Roses video for "You Could Be Mine". We were silently oppositional, yet maybe respectful of a remote yin and yang we knew might exist somehow. Around that time we would drink in the same local bars with different sets of friends, places where it wasn't uncommon for a drunken fight to break out after last call that involved multiple parties. It would have been more unlikely for a fight *not* to break out, really. I recall that during one of these Saturday night melees in particular, the gang of Sudbury Wolves hockey players I was with got into it with some other group of drunks. In the ensuing fracas, I found myself entangled with none other than my future pal Garvey, momentarily toe-to-toe and each holding the other's shirt with the threat of exchanging blows. In a single moment, we looked each other in the eye, let go, and stepped away as the fight raged on around us.

Our last year of university forced a union between us purely out of default. The only seat available in the psych class I had signed up for to earn my degree at Laurentian was directly beside Garvey. I can still see that visual in my mind, standing in the doorway right before the first class started, surveying a room replete with no one else I cared to commiserate with about how difficult it would be to earn a passing grade in this class. Garvey looked over at me with a vague smile and raised his eyebrows in the form of a polite greeting. I went over and sat down, and that was it.

We joined forces, and it was us against everyone else in that class. The demands of the curriculum that year urged us to rely on each other to do well, and we spent enough time together out of necessity to find out that the other guy wasn't so bad after all.

By the end of that year, we had planned to continue our studies together after graduation via a Master's degree in the States. We even had the schools earmarked - Ball State in Indiana topped the list. Tuition costs of twenty grand per year of study provided a roadblock, so I proposed to take a year off to work and generate the money. Garvey would go ahead and I would catch up with him the following year. Never did happen though. He went ahead to the University of Massachusetts for his Master's degree, and then on to Memphis and Florida to eventually earn his Doctorate in forensic psychology. I moved from Sudbury to Toronto and worked in finance for the duration of those years. I used to wonder how different my life would have been had I joined Garvey on that academic path we had initially scoped out together. It matters very little now, of course. What really mattered was that two individuals as oddly paired as we had seemed to be would retain a long-lasting friendship made even more unlikely and improbable by our chosen life paths, both now and then.

And now, look at this. So strange…

When I looked down at my iPod, I laughed to myself. Of all of the songs on my playlist, the timing of my next one seemed serendipitous. Couldn't have been any more perfect, really. It was "Shake Me" by Cinderella. The yin to Bruce Springsteen's yang.

I turned and looked at Garvey. "This song grabbed me by my three-quarter sleeve baseball jersey and threw my sixteen-year-old ass into the air," I said as the song triggered that familiar sensation I felt every time I heard it. This was a tune about the pleasures of the flesh, pure and simple. Its big, rude raw guitar chords sneered from the sound dock in the truest representation of the spirit of 80s hair rock.

Cinderella worked their way up through the Philadelphia bar scene, just a few miles over the Delaware River from where The Boss lamented his blue collar upbringing in New Jersey. The by-product of their intentions, regardless of sophistication or style, were in essence the same. They both delivered that special voltage of emotive electricity.

Way out here in the Canadian Rockies so many years later, Garvey and I both recognized the familiar power of that electricity and the rich emancipation that it brought, regardless of its musical source. The gratification we sought from it was the very thing that had united us all along. And be it Springsteen, Cinderella, or otherwise, it would be wholeheartedly celebrated out here now.

CHAPTER 8

And If You Don't Know, Now You Know

"Let's grill up those steaks," Garvey suggested. "And pack this stuff up and head inside. It's goddamn cold out here."

The sun, albeit having been behind the clouds for the past few hours, had now gone down. It was dark. The barbecue gazebo was well lit, however.

"Alright," I replied, gathering up all of the empties and potato chip bag refuse while Garvey unplugged the dock and carried it inside along with his iPod.

As we prepared our meal for the grill, I poured myself a couple of fingers of scotch. The combination of Garvey's voice and the act of pouring a drink triggered a memory.

"Garvey, did you want to mix me up a gimlet?" I asked. There was a story behind this comment.

During the summer immediately after we had graduated from Laurentian and before Garvey left for Massachusetts, we worked together at a resort in a tiny little town an hour south of Sudbury called Killarney, on the north channel of Georgian Bay. We had both been bestowed with responsibilities we probably shouldn't have been at that point in our lives. I managed the employees who received the yachts that docked at the resort, and Garvey somehow got a job as a bartender in the resort's lounge, despite the fact that he had no previous experience as a bartender of any description.

A lot of well-heeled folks from the States came through this resort on their way to Manitoulin Island, the largest fresh water island on the planet. The clientele ranged from sailboaters right up to owners of eighty and ninety foot yachts containing their own crews. Mostly though, it was wealthy executives or businesspeople on vacation with their families and friends. Both our roles with the resort required us to interact with most of these customers at some point during their stay, which was commensurate with the number of stories we took away from that summer.

So one afternoon a well-dressed older woman came into the lounge with her equally well-dressed older husband while Garvey was on shift at the bar. This would always make him a bit anxious, as his knowledge of the spirits beyond the conventional rye-and-Coke variety was represented by a book he kept open just below the bar. The woman approached him and ordered a gimlet with all manner of specifications and extras - dry, no this, extra that, and on and on. Very particular. So, Garvey resorted to his little recipe book under the bar while the woman waited. All was not lost in these situations however, because Garvey had enough charm and charisma to carry what may have been lacking in his inexperience as a bartender. This was likely why he was there in the first place. He was a smooth talker. People liked him.

This particular lady would form her own opinion, however.

After Garvey concocted what he thought was a pretty decent gimlet according to the specifications of his cheater manual, he handed it to the woman and she brought it over to the table where her husband was waiting for her. She sat down with him to enjoy the special treat that Garvey had just prepared.

Immediately upon taking her first drink, she bolted upright out of her chair and said something unintelligible to her husband, who then rose from his chair and started towards the door. The woman walked over to Garvey with the drink and put it down on the bar in front of him. She looked him in the eye and deadpanned, *'Don't ever try and make one of those again'*. With that, she stormed out of the lounge. The entire place went silent.

I regress into laughter recounting this story. Poor Garvey. That must have been horrible.

"Ah, fuck her," Garvey said flatly. "Who drinks goddamn *gimlets* in these times, anyway?"

I was dying. This response made me laugh harder.

"Okay, pull yourself together, you degenerate. This stuff's ready," Garvey announced as he gathered up our vegetables to take to the barbecue. Just a simple butter and salt & pepper application to the steaks. No need to fool around with them any further. I was already on my way out the door with them. I had to pay extra attention to how these would be cooked, as I didn't want to screw them up. We were well refreshed at this point.

"Wait for me, gay lover!" Garvey yelled sarcastically out the door to me in that stupid voice. I started laughing again and almost dropped the steaks on the grass.

"Keep it down, you jackass," I hissed.

"You said there would be no judgment!!" Garvey loudly continued in the voice. We were both laughing like fools.

He sat down with a bottle of wine he brought out as I looked over this barbecue's operating features, after having reached under the grill to open up the propane valve. I pushed the ignition button, craning my neck away from the grill. Then again, and again. Nothing. Then a very, very small line of blue and orange flames flickered beneath the grill.

"Must be low on propane," Garvey said. "That sucks."

"We should call the guy," I said, not knowing who the guy (or girl) was, or even if there was such a person we could call.

"I'll go over to the office and ask," Garvey advised and started walking in that direction into the darkness. After a few minutes, he re-emerged with another man. The guy.

"Hey," I greeted. "Thanks for coming over. I think we're low on propane." Garvey had likely already voiced this concern.

"Let's have a look," the guy offered.

He removed the tank from its position underneath the grill and shook it.

"Nope, plenty of propane," he declared.

I was perplexed by the fact that he was able to deduce the amount of propane in the cylinder by just waving it around as he did. He was probably just fucking with us, having already sized us up.

He reconnected the propane cylinder and performed some additional tweaking as Garvey and I stood with our arms folded, looking on like unengaged foremen at a construction site who pretended to be engaged.

"Not sure what to tell you. I'll have someone look at it tomorrow morning," the guy concluded.

"Thanks," was all I could muster. I felt somewhat defeated. The grill had looked as though it had just been used not long ago.

Garvey looked at me. "Pan fry?" he asked.

"Yeah. Screw this."

We headed back to the cabin, careful not to drop any of our edible cargo.

After dinner was sorted, it was back to the playlists. The sound dock hadn't stopped working over the course of our meal. During that time we had been listening to My Morning Jacket, I think. Maybe Johnny Marr.

"Whose turn is it?" Garvey asked.

"Not sure," I replied. "Go ahead."

Garvey inserted his iPod into the dock and walked over to the armchair that would serve as his permanent outpost over the course of our time here. I was already in mine, a similar armchair next to the sofa that opposed his diagonally. The sound dock was positioned on a table against the wall on the other side of the room, but less than seven feet from both our seats. The fireplace was on my left beyond the sofa. In this dimly lit space, we were prepared to enter the next phase of this experience.

Garvey's song started with someone tuning their guitar. Had to be Neil Young.

"Here we have "Down by the River" live at the Fillmore, Neil Young and Crazy Horse," he said.

"At his best, Neil Young's guitar playing is all about feeling," Garvey hypothesized as Young choppily soloed through one of the lengthy instrumental passages "Down by the River" was known for. "Clearly it's not about technique, but as a shitty guitar player, this stuff inspires me."

"Neil's one-note guitar solo in "Cinnamon Girl" has earned him a lot of respect from a lot of guitar players, including Kim Thayil from Soundgarden," I added. I didn't care that much about Soundgarden, or one-note guitar solos. I preferred Neil's acoustic stuff.

"Yeah," Garvey responded. "He's got that special feel. This song really showcases that."

I had never heard this version of "Down by the River" before, and I eventually had to acknowledge that Young's lead playing was in fact a bit better than I had originally thought. Here was another dichotomous fork in the road for Garvey and me - the difference in understanding and appreciation of the guitar solo.

I was inspired by fleet-fingered speedsters with equal parts flash and technical skill, recognizing that the guitar solo was often the crescendo of a song. Like it was with Jake E. Lee's blistering lead in Ozzy Osbourne's "Bark at the Moon", for example. I had been thrilled by these demonstrations of virtuosity as a young kid, and quite honestly they still make me frothy with excitement. So, it was my natural inclination to sniff at Young's paltry note usage in his lead playing, the same mostly off-key notes being strangled over and over again. I had been conditioned to do this. But this was one of the reasons why I was here. Not only to listen, but also to deepen my appreciation for the other sides of the story.

Interestingly enough, the next song on my playlist began with a guitar solo.

"What song starts with a guitar solo like this?" I asked Garvey.

It struck me at that moment as unusual, though I'm sure it hadn't been the first time in the history of rock and roll that it had happened.

"Ah, "Reelin' in the Years". Very nice," Garvey said. "Interesting choice for you. What gives?"

"Steely Dan came along at a time in my life when I was looking for a bit more tranquility," I responded. "Their music strikes you as a muzak-ish version of jazz when you first hear it, but there's a wry subtlety in there when you really listen to the tight musicianship and the lyrics. It's like we were saying earlier about 70s music. The instrumentation has a bouncy, soothing quality about it, but the lyrics are sardonic and cutting. Their first record, *Can't Buy a Thrill*, is loaded with great songs, and this is one of 'em. And, the band is named after a vibrator."

This little factoid had absolutely nothing to do with my previous comments about the band's music, but I thought I'd throw it in. It was true.

"What?" Garvey questioned.

"Yeah. William Burroughs' *Naked Lunch* novel, back in the 50s I think. A vibrator is named Steely Dan by one of the characters."

"Hmmm. Didn't know that."

"Well if you don't know, now you know."

"Huh?"

"Notorious B.I.G., man. Come on."

I actually know very little about Notorious B.I.G. or his music. I'm only familiar with this lyric because it's taken on a meme-like quality in our society. And also because I follow Bianca Kajlich on Twitter.

"You're up, man," I said to Garvey from my chair, wondering what would emerge from his playlist next. It was Pink Floyd, with their clever lyrics about human longing and self-deception. Talented group, but I never really understood Pink Floyd.

"This is a musical onomatopoeia. The song sounds like floating. It's ethereal. And the David Gilmour guitar solo is maybe the most beautiful, melodic solo in rock," Garvey declared.

"That's a very bold statement, sir," I observed.

"I stand by it."

I liked that about Garvey. He didn't just make wild, off-the-cuff claims that he wasn't prepared to back up. I didn't agree with his assertion about Gilmour's solo, but I didn't discount it either.

My next tune would shake up the proceedings a bit. It was Metallica's "Ride the Lightning" track from the album of the same name.

"This song makes me feel like I can pick up that Honda outside with my bare hands and throw it over Castle Mountain," I told Garvey. "This was thrash metal with groove, back when James Hetfield didn't sing in tenor. Seems like a lifetime ago."

"Yep," Garvey nodded. "It really does."

I was confused and impressed when Garvey took the time to learn Metallica's "Seek and Destroy" on the guitar a few years back, a song that used to make my non-metalhead friends wince with displeasure. Watching him play it back then was mildly jarring. These were all representations I thought I had left behind as time wore on. But I'm not sure we ever really completely free ourselves of these thoughts at any point.

The song Garvey put on next reinforced my joy in having put this whole exercise together. It was a song by The Monks, called "Johnny B. Rotten".

Garvey smiled as he explained. "Early pop-punk. It just sounds like rock and roll should, y'know?"

"Yes, I do," I said as I listened.

I loved the singer's sneering Cockney accent. It reminded me of Squeeze's "Cool For Cats". My familiarity with The Monks began and ended with their "Drugs in my Pocket" single, but I appreciated the grass-roots appeal of this track. It made me consider buying the record, actually.

My turn. I *ka-chiked* my iPod into the dock, pushed play on Jet's "Look What You've Done", and walked over to the other side of the room to start a fire. Garvey furled his brow in a way Jean-Luc Picard may have.

"What's the band?" he asked.

"Jet. This is from their first record, *Get Born*, the one with "Are You Gonna Be My Girl?" on it.

"Right. What's the attraction?"

"For me, it's really pretty amazing how just those two introductory piano notes can hang such a haunting pall over your head before the song even starts. But when it does, it's just perfect. The melody is heartfelt, the instrumentation isn't overbearing, and the track doesn't try too hard to wring sentimentality out of you like a lot of newer rock does. And it's got that sly wink to The Beatles in there with that electric guitar lick in the chorus. I love this song. This is actually a great record. And this band, if we're being honest…"

"And we are," Garv interjected.

"This band actually got me excited about rock again after I heard this record, in the sense that it marked the first time since I was a teenager that I was actually excited about a band's upcoming release of their next album."

"And…?"

I exhaled.

"It simply was not to be. I felt like they flew a little too close to the Beatles and Oasis suns, y'know? Like a musical Icarus, they burned their wings and plummeted back to earth. I didn't like the second album at all," I responded. "I think there's a lot of pressure on these new bands today, and it impairs any long-term sustainability. That growth and development window isn't there anymore, like it was for bands like Def Leppard or U2."

"Or The Rolling Stones," Garvey responded, shoving his iPod into the dock after removing mine. The rough, organic acoustic guitar chords of *Sticky Fingers*' "Sister Morphine" filled the room.

"This is a black, haunting love song to Jagger's mistress. Dark and brooding, but still somehow exciting," Garvey postulated.

"I feel like this is a peculiar song that could have only been written during that time, with that effected slide guitar. It's a bit too long for my liking," I pointed out. "Sister Morphine" was never one of my favourites from an album I otherwise absolutely loved.

"Screw you, Jensen," Garvey mocked as he pulled out his iPod and I put mine in. We were punching our time cards at the musical appreciation factory. The paychecks came in the learning.

Up next was one of the true kings of the musical frontier as I saw it, and this was one of my favourite songs of his. "Quicksand", from David Bowie.

Garvey smiled pensively. "I knew Bowie would eventually make his appearance on your playlist," he said.

"I do love Mister Bowie."

David Bowie was one of a handful of pure singer-songwriters in his day, and the brilliant album this song comes from, *Hunky Dory*, is his first real demonstration of that fact.

"I could have picked a number of songs from this record - "Life on Mars", "Changes", "Oh! You Pretty Things". Maybe "Queen Bitch". Actually, some of those may be included somewhere else in my playlist," I went on. "But this song is special. It's master class songwriting, lyrically and musically. Despairing and hopeful at the same time."

The words broke in my throat a bit as I detailed my affinity for this song. I'd been mildly choked up talking about more than a few of my songs up to this point, actually. I was just so thrilled to be able to personally represent them in this forum, as a real extension of myself, that I actually found it difficult to speak without having my voice crack periodically through segments of our conversation. But this meant something important. This was why I was here.

CHAPTER 9

Super Prostitute

"The whole *Black Sheep* record is brilliant. This was Sexton's last album before the record company started overproducing everything he did. Plus, this song includes these great lines: '*loving you is like loving a house on fire*', and '*loving you is like loving a fifth of the finest bourbon*'," Garvey said of the selection he was currently playing, Martin Sexton's "Can't Stop Thinking 'Bout You".

I hadn't been familiar, but I actually really liked this Martin Sexton stuff. It was rich with style and substance. Flecks of Billie Holliday and Ray Charles. I found out later that Sexton was actually white, which surprised me. This sure as hell didn't sound like a white kid from Boston to me. I had suspected Garvey's list would provide a bit of education to me during this exercise, and it certainly had so far. I was sucking this stuff up like a sponge.

With his music, Garvey had taken a different path than I had. His playlist was nothing at all like mine. Lots of Motown, old blues, vintage soul numbers. Artists I'd heard of but had never really followed up on. People whose names periodically emerge and then immediately recede back into the musical ether. People like Al Green.

Garvey had the benefit of having an uncle that served almost as a music 'pusher', a connection who had hooked him up with stuff like Martin Sexton, Ike and Tina, and Steely Dan, at a time in his life when he was young and hungry for it. I was reliant on my own wits, just lapping up easy superficial things that had been right in front of me. I came in through the 80s hard rock front door and had to learn rock genealogy in reverse - I didn't really find out about these older, greater acts until years later. But as a teenager I really didn't care to find out, because I felt like that kind of music was for older people. I purposely misinformed myself, even in the face of the fact that these artists I ignored were the same ones that influenced the bands I listened to and loved at that time. I knew that. But I didn't *want* to know back then. I was a distressed, petulant kid who lacked better influences. As I got older and more appreciative, that mindset changed drastically. Soon I wanted to know everything. And now, out here, I wanted to know even more.

Garvey and I had worshipped at the same altar of musical appreciation after I broadened my scope back in the late 80s, and that kind of worship doesn't recognize genre boundaries. We always belonged to the same tribe, and in essence this was why we were such good friends. And all these years later, now it seemed Garvey might be regarded as my pusher in a sense.

I had always admired his assuredness. The peace he had inside. He didn't seem to host any of the damage that I carried around, that same damage a good number of these songs amplified. This was what contrasted us in my mind. Music didn't haunt him the same way it haunted me, and I wanted to know why. I had come out here looking for answers, having a handful of pieces I was trying to fit together hoping that this excursion would provide the last one to complete the puzzle. And now things were becoming clearer. This was turning into something else now. I began to realize that it was peace I was after, the same peace Garvey had.

I didn't have to be relieved when the next song on my playlist was not Ratt's "Wanted Man", but I still was. Joni Mitchell's "Free Man in Paris" came up instead.

Yes, she paired nicely with the newspaper and coffee on Saturday mornings, but Joni Mitchell represented far more value beyond simple background music commodification. Her songs brought me back to my youth, aligning themselves with other earlier childhood memories and providing a softer echo of nostalgic calm. Maybe this was why I refused to listen to Mitchell after dark. Dark was for later on in my younger life. Dark was for rage - for Slayer and Motley Crue and the emergence of my teenage rebellion against the world. Who needs a psychologist when music can provide a Rorschach guide through your emotional topography?

Seconds before "Free Man in Paris" ended, I ran over to the dock and yanked out my iPod before it could reveal my next song.

"Almost showed my next card there," I exhaled.

Garvey's turn now.

"I hate jazz, but I love this record," he said. "This first track creeps up and envelops you. Perfect for either background or headphone listening." It was Miles Davis' "Blue is Green", from the album *Kind of Blue*.

"But what does it make you feel?" I asked.

"It provides the same calm to me that Joni Mitchell provides to you," Garvey replied.

I listened in ambivalence to the shrill trumpet at first, uncomfortable with all of the unexciting impressions similar trumpet jazz lines had left in my head in the past. I didn't much care for jazz, and cared even less for people who included jazz in their music collections as a means of displaying a cultural sophistication they wanted you to think they actually had. What I did like about this music was the uncertainty and the lack of structure - there was no defined beginning or end. It was amorphous; listless and vague, just kind of floating in panorama without any real structure at all. There was a purity in that idea. Maybe also a mild form of peril. And I liked that.

I may have heard these things before, but I didn't really *listen* to them. I knew they were there all along, but now they were being presented to me and I had no choice but to experience them from start to finish. The education continued.

"Well done, Garvin. If the rest of your playlist inspires me the way it has up to this point, you may be going home without an iPod," I told him.

He smiled, nodded his head downward and raised his glass.

"You're up."

I looked at my next selection and gasped a little. Garvey looked up at me. This was definitely a nighttime song. AC/DC's "Sin City".

"*Wake up!*" I yelled as the pulverizing guitar chords leapt from the sound dock like some violent alarm. This was a live version of the song with Brian Johnson singing and not Bon Scott, and the song was that much more uptempo and aggressive. This aggression was lent additional power by the softness of our previous selections. Playing these all of these songs alongside each other seemed perverse and brilliant at the same time.

"This has always been my favourite AC/DC song. When I finally upgraded my university stereo to include some Paradigm speakers in senior year, this tune blasted through the halls of our dorm several times every Saturday night. It was like our battle cry," I recalled.

"I think this song was a battle cry for most of the drinking community of Sudbury," Garvey added. This was a substantial portion of Sudbury's population.

"Before I die, I need to hear Axl Rose sing "Sin City" live. In fact, I refuse to die until I hear it," I said.

Garvey's next selection, "The Night They Drove Old Dixie Down" by The Band, slowed the tempo right back down again. This was a song I never really liked that much, being the lousy Canadian that I am. I'm not sure why, but I just didn't care for this song. Could have been the vocal, I don't know.

"Ever see *The Last Waltz*, the documentary from Martin Scorcese?" Garvey asked.

I nodded in the negative.

"It was The Band's farewell concert, at the Winterland Ballroom in San Francisco," he explained.

My only familiarity with the Winterland Ballroom came from the black and white KISS bootleg of one of their *Hotter Than Hell* tour concerts. It was shot at the Winterland in early 1975, back when Gene Simmons was almost as skinny as Ace Frehley.

"There are a bunch of other Canadians guesting on this, in addition to people like Bob Dylan, Ringo Starr, and Ronnie Wood. You have Neil Young, Ronnie Hawkins, your pal Joni Mitchell and some others, and they make you feel a certain amount of pride. Anthemic and proud. That's what this is. I love this," Garvey said.

I appreciated the sentiment, but hearing the song again didn't change anything for me. Besides, it would have been weird if I had loved every song that Garvey played. I was naturally expecting not to, just as I was expecting that he would dislike a good number of my selections.

Turns out he liked the next one though - Aerosmith's "Seasons of Wither". The haunting, swirling wind effect that could be heard in the intro was intensified by our surroundings, out in the darkness of the woods.

"Like most of the older Aerosmith ballads, this song feels wounded. Like it doesn't quite get to where it's trying to go. I like that, because it feels more real that way," I said. "For me, this song's appeal lies in its vulnerability. It's completely polarized by New Aerosmith's super polished, more technically crafted pop singles. "Seasons of Wither" is perfectly demonstrative of that schism between Old Aerosmith and New Aerosmith. And I'll take my Aerosmith *old*, please. I feel like the new stuff isn't nearly as substantial."

"Why don't you just come out and say what you really feel?" Garvey chided.

"Oh, I will. Especially if a Clapton song turns up in your playlist," I replied.

"That's a distinct possibility," Garvey said through his wine glass. "Now get your goddamn iPod out of there, it's my turn."

"Hallelujah" was his next selection, and it sounded like Jeff Buckley's version. I'd never been terribly interested in this song, which is likely a sin in a lot of people's minds.

"This song is as beautiful as "Amazing Grace". People will sing it a century from now. This is Jeff Buckley's version, but I could have just as easily played Leonard Cohen's," Garvey stated. He was right.

"Never really cared for it," I said. "It just always seems overwrought."

Garvey squinted at me like I was trying to poison him. He shook his head in disapproval of my comment. I absorbed his disappointment, but I had to be honest.

My comfort was restored by my next selection. "Wise Up", by Aimee Mann. I found this song to be profoundly heartbreaking. And I did find comfort in the substance of legitimately heartbreaking music.

"Nice pick. Aimee Mann?" Garvey asked.

"Yep. From the *Magnolia* soundtrack," I said. "*No, no, no.* Sorry, this is from the *American Beauty* soundtrack," I asserted. Loosened lips.

"Both great movies," Garvey observed. "Either way, this song could have easily made *Magnolia*'s soundtrack."

"No question. I think that may have been why I said it. It almost sounds like it could have been written specifically for *Magnolia*. *Magnolia* is an incredible movie, isn't it?" I continued. "It doesn't seem so much like a movie as a reminder of real life pathos, the real regret that's lurking back there behind people's elaborate facades. The way the movie frames the disappointment of life makes it almost hard to watch," I said.

We needed to veer away from the darkened path we were currently on.

Our playlists were working together with the wine to drain our power. I was approaching a low point, and I hoped that the next song would be upbeat, raucous. Some Van Halen maybe. Hell, I'd have taken Bananarama at this point.

But neither of these came. Instead, from Garvey's iPod came James Taylor.

Argh.

After a moment this actually caused me to laugh, thus clearing away some of the fog that had settled in around us. I laughed because of the irony of Garvey's song order as it related to my musical taste. I did not care for James Taylor's music, at all. He was like my musical Kryptonite in times like this.

When I had satellite radio, I would tune in to the 70s station in the hopes of catching something like Nazareth's "Bad, Bad Boy" or Nick Gilder's "Hot Child in the City", but it was like James Taylor's mother was the program director of this station - James Taylor song after James Taylor song would play, forcing me to adjust the dial. To me, Taylor's music represented that cloying, sleepy syrup that often casts 70s music in an unfavourable light. And now here he was, the third of three consecutive songs on Garvey's playlist that I had not cared for. The chances of this happening made me laugh out loud.

"What's funny?" Garvey asked.

I explained my perception to him. "I've tried to like James Taylor, I really have. He comes from the same place as a lot of other artists I do like. But his style just makes me want to snuff it," I reasoned.

"It's not for everybody," Garvey allowed.

The song was called "Something in the Way She Moves", with Carole King, recorded live from The Troubadour. "I think Taylor has a gorgeous, unique voice. He writes heartfelt songs, and he plays guitar with this really beautiful finger-picking style."

"No judgment. And I can see all that. This song actually seems like a bit of a departure from his usual stuff. Just not my thing, that's all."

There was legitimacy in disagreement between me and Garvey. Over the years I could always depend on him to tell me the truth, even when I didn't necessarily want to hear it. It was a trait of his I had always respected. It disappointed me when people wouldn't provide honest, constructive feedback in favour of taking the easier complimentary road. We both knew where we stood with each other.

"Only Women Bleed" by Alice Cooper was my next selection. Not quite so upbeat in terms of sentiment, but at least the song's tempo would pick things up somewhat around the middle eight.

I looked over at Garvey. "I've always loved that delicate guitar line that starts this track. Alice was a master of mood manipulation in his songs, through both the music and the lyrical messages. His songs always seemed so vast. Alice was like Zeppelin in this way. He didn't necessarily limit himself to one musical genre, because for him it was more about expression through music, not the other way around. Know what I mean?"

"Yeah, definitely."

"I think Alice's genius back then was that his brand was in fact *not* having a definable musical brand per se. Think about such a shiny hit single like "No More Mr. Nice Guy" being on the same album as something like "Sick Things" or "I Love the Dead". Vincent Furnier's brand was Alice Cooper, which reached beyond any specific musical genre. This sounds easier to pull off than it actually was. Other similar acts like KISS tried, but they failed."

Garvey nodded slowly without speaking, looking at the floor while he pushed my words around in his mind.

The statistical probability that I would not dislike his next song was that much greater this time. I braced a little right before he pressed play.

Ah, yes. I did like this. Tom Petty and Stevie Nicks doing "Stop Dragging My Heart Around".

"A dark, call-and-response duet sung by two unique voices, performed as beleaguered lovers," Garvey summarized.

"I like this," I said, without intending direct appeasement. This song brought a warm familiarity that Garvey likely also felt.

As Petty and Nicks adjusted our atmosphere inside the chalet, I ruminated through the pitfalls of what we were doing here. While I respected the requirement for randomness and an absence of structure, the intention being to wildly throw our selections out there without regard for any kind of flow, I did have some concern for the imbalance that could result here. I worried about the potential for a lull to be brought on by a fluke combination of songs, his and mine together, that could combine to form a helix of lethargy that would put us both to sleep. I needed an ass-shaker at this point. I felt like we needed to lift this thing up.

I reached over the table for my iPod and looked at it. Damn. No ass-shaker this time. Next up for me was the ever-doomy "Rooster", by Alice in Chains.

Great. Alice in Chains guitarist Jerry Cantrell's sombre means of connecting with his Vietnam vet father. I locked in and pressed play, unleashing singer Layne Staley's blackness into our already darkened space.

Garvey's next song stood in direct contrast with "Rooster", as most of his songs would with mine. It was a blues tune woven together with a shrill guitar lead that seemed to have inspired Keith Richards' solo in "Sympathy for the Devil".

"Who's this?" I asked.

"This is Freddie King," Garvey said.

Didn't ring a bell, unless I misunderstood 'B.B.' to be 'Freddie'.

"The song is called "Going Down", Garvey said. "It makes me tap my foot and really punch the gas pedal when I'm driving. To me, the song actually feels like plummeting earthward. It's got some of the earliest rock god guitar playing on it."

I had always been interested in the genealogy of blues guitar players and how these men had ushered in a phalanx of guitar gods of their own, guys like Keith Richards, Jeff Beck, Jimmy Page, and on and on down the line. I had never really familiarized myself with this lineage outside of an opaque awareness of players like Son House, Muddy Waters, Howlin' Wolf, Robert Johnson - you know, the ones you always hear about. Garvey's time spent in the American South likely had contributed to this heightened awareness in this area. I was appreciative that he was sharing this with me now.

My turn again.

Upbeat? Not exactly. "Here, There, and Everywhere", a Sir Paul composition from The Beatles' tremendous *Revolver* record.

I always thought the *Revolver* album cover was highly prescient - John's image on the right side, looking calculating and devious, peering side-eyed at Paul's image on the left, which was petulant in response. Between their faces in the middle of the album cover's illustration were representations of all the little things that both united and separated them. It was perfect, whether intentional or not.

"I can honestly say that the beauty of this melody stopped me in my tracks the very first time I heard it. The ascending line, the background vocal accompaniment, it's incredible," I said. "Reason number forty-six why Paul McCartney is the most prolific songwriter in the history of popular music."

This was a relatively bold claim to make, but I'd made it in the past and vehemently stood by it. In my mind, no one compares to Macca.

Garvey did not refute my claim. Instead, he wordlessly removed my iPod from the dock at the conclusion of the song and inserted his own, which may have been considered a bit blasphemous by some.

Another blues tune from him.

""Boom Boom", John Lee Hooker," Garvey announced. "Simple stuff. Just a blues lick and a voice that seems like it carries the weight of the world."

I did enjoy Garvey's perceptions of these songs, his descriptions explaining why they stirred him the way they did. I noted how completely attuned he was with how he felt about his favourite music. How he could always verbalize these feelings with such facility.

I got up and walked over to the sound dock, hoping that my next selection would strike some uptempo oil. I almost felt like one of those older women sitting in front of their Vegas slot machines, wearing Depends so that nature's call could not come between them and their coveted jackpot, hope increasingly eclipsed by growing desperation with every pull of the lever. The twisted, weird desperation they must have felt.

I almost felt like that. But not nearly so dire. I could step away to use the bathroom any time I wanted. My payout wasn't going anywhere.

I did need it to come soon though.

Finally, with my next pull, it would be delivered. An upbeat song at last came up in my playlist, one over which Garvey and I could share a sentimental laugh - Billy Squier's "The Stroke". I smiled in reverence.

"Here's a nice little number for you," I yelled over that unmistakeable kick and snare drum combination that introduced the track. The initiative of this song filled the room. Back in business.

"*Nice!*" Garvey piped up. "This is a great tune." It was like an old friend of ours had walked through the door.

Squier's bombast revitalized me. I gulped the last of the wine from my glass and nodded enthusiastically along to the groove.

"I remember the first time I heard this song back when I was twelve years old. I was in the back seat of the family car in the parking lot of a grocery store, hypnotized by what I was hearing. It was so catchy and foreign, with those big background vocals and the sinister keyboard in the breakdown near the end of the song. It sounded like a bizarre call-to-arms military anthem for some sexual revolution I couldn't know about yet. I ran out and bought the 45 and played it incessantly," I gushed.

"Very similar memories of that song, yes. I loved it too," Garvey said.

And with that, fresh new life filled our chalet. A second wind.

As it turned out, Garvey's next selection granted an extended walk down the memory lane of 1981. It was "Super Freak" by Rick James. What were the chances of this? I howled in approval of this serendipity.

"Dude, did you know that "The Stroke" and "Super Freak" both came out in 1981?" I exclaimed.

I was ninety-three percent sure of this fact, an estimation that always rounds up to a full one hundred percent when the booze is flowing.

"No. You sure about that?" Garvey questioned.

"One hundred percent."

See? It does.

Garvey consulted his iPhone. "Well, what the fuck do you know about that?!?" he confirmed. "That's crazy."

Had I been under the influence of narcotics, my mind would have certainly concocted some form of conspiracy theory to explain the coincidence. It was a bit strange that our lists seem to be undulating in a strange synchronicity with each other.

"So - "Super Freak"?" I looked at Garv.

"Yeah. This is dirty, dirty, dirty funk. All the innuendo of old school soul, but worn on the outside," he responded.

"I listened to this a lot as a kid, but not as much as "The Stroke"," I said. "I remember hearing on some TV program that 'freak' was slang for prostitute, and so the song kinda put me on my heels a bit. It weirded me out that Rick James was telling me about a Super Prostitute. These concepts were too big for me as a younger kid."

"Joining a sexual 'stroke' revolution was okay, but hearing about a prostitute was too much for you?" Garvey asked.

"*Super* prostitute, Garvey," I corrected. "A super hooker was extra dangerous, and using the word 'super' and 'prostitute' together messed with my mind back then. I had only just stopped reading comic books and watching *Superfriends* cartoons on TV at that time, and the fact that an untoward sex worker could exist inside the innocent make-believe world of superhero comics was menacing and unpalatable to me as a twelve year old. Even if I did have a little thing for Batgirl."

"Little indeed. Your turn, weirdo," Garvey said.

I popped my iPod in and pushed play on one of the most soothing songs I've ever heard. The Black Crowes' "Wiser Time".

"Beautiful. Absolutely beautiful," Garvey responded.

"Just so lush and calming, huh? I feel like this music belongs to me. I love that little cowbell double tap at the end of every measure," I said.

"The whole thing, man. The instruments are just so artfully played, and everything just flows together so nicely."

A warm glow emanated through our chalet now, fire crackling and booze flowing. Alcohol and song had now fully intertwined themselves in the devil's bargain, a feeling that was ethereal and familiar. I inhaled and waited for Garvey's next selection.

"Gimme something good, Garvin," I said quietly.

"Here you go. Let's keep this groove going."

The Temptations poured forth from the sound dock. Very nice.

"This is "I Wish It Would Rain". David Ruffin had a great, growly voice. It makes everything sound so sincere and profound," Garvey said.

"Sweet. Have you ever seen that made-for-TV movie about Ruffin and The Temptations?" I asked. "Dude was a motherfucker, man."

"No, I don't think so."

"I think they took some liberties with some of the actual facts, but the whole story is really compelling. It focuses mostly on Ruffin's ego and the drug problems he had after the band made it. After a series of missed shows and ruffled feathers with the group and Barry Gordy, they threw Ruffin out and replaced him with another guy. But Ruffin went to their shows and when they played Ruffin-era numbers, he jumped up on the stage and took the microphone out of the new guy's hands and sang the songs, and the crowd would freak out. Then Ruffin begged the band to take him back, even though he's still a mess. It's pathetic and unsettling to witness."

"His whole descent is pretty unsettling," Garvey responded.

"True. Great singer though. Shame."

My playlist contained its first artist double-play at this point, prompting another Black Crowes tune - this time from the brilliant *The Southern Harmony and Musical Companion* record. It was "Bad Luck Blue Eyes Goodbye".

"Sorry, I'm repeating the Crowes. No song list order."

"Don't ever be sorry about playing two Black Crowes songs in a row," Garvey replied.

"That guitar lick sequence, dude...," I started while guitarist Marc Ford's weary lead played over Rich Robinson's F# minor to A chord sequence. I didn't finish. I just shook my head. It was my favourite part of this entire album.

I looked over at Garvey. His eyes were closed, his mouth forming a contented smile in appreciation of this song. He could feel it too. Of course he could.

He arose from his chair after the song ended and walked over to the sound dock, looking first at his iPod and then up at me with raised eyebrows and a smile.

"Believe it or not, we have another band double-play," he said, and pushed play. And with that, those tense, unmistakeable bars of hi-hat notes kicked off The Temptations' "Papa Was A Rolling Stone".

"The Temptations sounded less doo-wop pretty and more street level gritty as they matured. This is like East Coast Sly and the Family Stone. It's pure 70s funk," Garvey observed.

"Well said. Nice selection."

Things were about to take a drastic turn.

My iPod indicated to me that "Overlord" was my next tune, from heavy metal lunatic Zakk Wylde and his Black Label Society. We were swerving into a hard right, away from soul and towards heavy metal.

Or were we?

Wylde's quieted wah pedal riff announced the challenge we were about to face. Garvey's brow furled. "What is *this*?"

As I opened my mouth to answer, Wylde's riff shed the wah effect and increased in volume, blasting out of the dock like a hurricane.

I felt that jolt again. The vibration in my skin.

"This is "Overlord", Black Label Society," I said.

Garvey squinted, confirming he'd been bitten by the beast.

"Somewhat of a transition from The Temptations, but listen closely to that riff. You can hear the groove. It's really funk, between the bookends of big distorted chords at the end of the measure. At his core, Zakk is a blues player, and he understands groove. Strip the distortion and the focus on heaviness in the production away, and this is a funky blues riff. Watch," I said as I got up and pressed pause on my iPod, then reached for the Gibson acoustic a few feet away.

I sat down with the guitar in my lap and played the eight notes of the "Overlord" riff, focusing on that string bend from B to C, without those pounding double-stop A and E chords that added the crushing metal effect. That bend was what made the riff funky and groovy.

"Imagine this being played by Rick James. It would sound super freaky, baby," I declared. "You wouldn't even have to change the tempo or the time signature. "Overlord" is a funk song hidden inside heavy metal packaging."

Of course, this isn't the only metal song that could be deconstructed in this way. But it's easy and tempting to listen only with the ears, and not with the mind. I was aware that Garvey knew this stuff. He likely just didn't care for the need for it.

"Why not just come out and play a funk song then?" he snorted.

"Why? Because you have to be who you are."

It felt like I wasn't saying this to Garvey so much as I was saying it to myself.

CHAPTER 10

Free Men in Paris

"See? It's all coming together now," I announced as that classic bass riff from Michael Jackson's "Billie Jean" made the table vibrate just a little bit. Garvey's next selection naturally perpetuated my funk argument. Our playlists were somehow in league with each other.

"Listen to the notes," I yelled over to Garvey's chair. "This riff is also in F# minor. If you sped up the tempo of "Overlord", the riff would fit right in there!" I was absolutely thrilled by the prospect of this.

Garvey, not so much.

"It's all connected!" I shouted.

"I'm afraid it wouldn't make much of a medley," he deadpanned.

"Maybe not in the same way as that '*come on everybody*' crap," I responded, referring to that unfortunate Jive Bunny and the Mastermixers remix monstrosity that combined Chubby Checker's "Let's Twist Again" with "Rock Around the Clock", "Tutti Fruitti", and "Wake Up Little Susie" back in the late 80s.

"But if you were playing one of these songs live, and you segued into the other via these riffs, it would be cool," I reasoned.

"I'd never play either one of these songs live," Garvey sniffed.

His band played mostly originals when they played bars at this juncture, but this was beside the point. He wouldn't do it regardless.

"I totally would. Segue from "Overlord" into "Billie Jean" in the breakdown and back again. Think about that, man. It would be amusing, at the very least."

"In my opinion, "Billie Jean" is maybe the best pop song ever written. Almost unquestionably, the best bass line ever written. Best not to screw around with stuff like that."

"Ah, come on."

There were no rules here.

"We could even mix in a little Black Sabbath if you fancied it," I kept up, pressing play to introduce my next song, Sabbath's "The Writ".

Garvey smirked but said nothing.

"This is my favourite Black Sabbath song, from my favourite Black Sabbath record."

Garvey was being patient with me now. Morning wasn't far off and I was getting a bit obnoxious. I elected to focus on rationalizing my song choice rather than wind him up.

"Okay, listen to Ozzy's voice on this. He hasn't sung with that much emotive power since 1977," I said. "He's making me actually believe it."

"Yeah," Garvey offered. "You're right. Doesn't sound at all like him. And that's a good thing."

I laughed. "Poor old Ozzy," I cracked in my best Sharon Osbourne brogue.

Garvey's next song would move us into a completely new area. I didn't know who was singing it, but I definitely knew the song. I loved the Toronto folk-rock band Leslie Spit Treeo's version of it so much that this song, along with the Spit's other big single, "UFO (Catch The Highway)", appeared on virtually every mix tape I made during the year of 1990.

"Ah, "Angel from Montgomery"!" I proclaimed. "I love this song. Who's doing this version?"

"Susan Tedeschi," Garvey answered. "This is just standalone beautiful. It's a woman feeling trapped in her life and wishing she could just fly away. There are several hall of fame versions of this song. There's John Prine's original, a testament to his songwriting skill that he was able to write this song from a woman's perspective. There's also Bonnie Raitt's, and there's this one by Sue Tedeschi. I chose Tedeschi's because she has one of my favourite female singing voices."

I didn't bother to ask Garvey if he had heard the Leslie Spit Treeo version of "Angel from Montgomery". I felt like it wouldn't matter much.

I sat back and listened to the final strains of Tedeschi's voice as the song concluded.

"Got another double," I advised, looking up at Garv from the screen of my iPod. I *ka-chiked* into the dock after Garvey punched out, and Sabbath's "Planet Caravan" softly emerged. I took my place in my listening chair.

"This song makes me feel like I'm walking on the moon underwater," I explained.

"There's something very ethereally special about it. It seems to just freeze everything in my periphery into this mellow, slow-motion countenance. It's definitely a headphones track."

"I know this tune," Garvey offered. "I think I had this album."

"Really? *Paranoid*?"

"Yeah, I think so."

"This song is just fantastic. I made a playlist a while back wherein I just had this song repeating seven times in a row, with the intention of hearing it a few times as I fell asleep. I was in a hotel room in Charlotte last year and I put it on around four in the morning after the night ended, and I was out. My friends next door told me the next day they considered breaking the door down to turn it off after the sixth consecutive play. I had the volume up a little high. Headphones next time," I said.

After "Planet Caravan" ended we would be treading into unusual territory. At least for me. Garvey's next selection was his most surprising yet. But I did enjoy this element of the enterprise.

"This is a goddamn beautiful song in its original, stripped down version. There are few things less cool than Carole King, but she's a bloody amazing singer songwriter." Garvey was adamant. "This one song represents the whole record. If we were doing records, I definitely would have included this one."

The record he was talking about was *Tapestry*, and the song he had chosen to represent it was "Natural Woman".

"I almost had "It's Too Late" from *Tapestry* on my playlist," I said. "But it joined "Send in the Clowns" on the bench."

Garvey's face lit up. "Which version? The Judy Collins one?"

"Yep. I remember seeing the song performed by Barbra Streisand on an awards show. Might have been the Grammys. I was really young. And you know, they did these musical representations back then on those shows where they more or less acted out the intended meaning of the song with a lot of dramatic flair, right?"

"Yeah, I remember."

"They may do similar things now, but it seemed quite different back then. More pathos, less flash, y'know? Anyway, this routine they had worked out seemed so sad. The song ended with a single clown, standing solemnly looking down at the floor off in the distance. He looked so small, a solitary sad spotlight shining down on him on an otherwise blacked out stage. I was only five or six then, but that really stayed with me. It seemed so tragic and lonely. Anyway, sorry - yes, Carole King."

"No, I think I saw that too. It almost made my list as well," Garvey said.

The thought of that song and that visual, still vivid in my mind, triggered something I wanted to come back to later. I had to put it aside for now, and focus on the present situation.

"I actually have a double-play here, but not of the artist variety. May I change the format up in light of this?" Garvey asked.

I was intrigued.

"Please, sir. Of course. Continue."

He advanced the playlist to his next song. It was "Natural Woman" again, this time featuring the unmistakeable voice of Aretha Franklin.

"I chose this song to show the contrast with Carole King's version. The song structure remains the same but the orchestration, the arrangement and Aretha's vocals turn it into something else," Garvey said.

"You're right. Interesting," I responded.

"And the coloured girls say, *'ah-oomph'*."

I admired Garvey's guts in choosing this song. I wasn't sure I knew anyone else who would have included "Natural Woman" in such a self-representative collection of songs. There were no contrivances in his playlist. No bullshit. I asked for what he felt and he was giving it to me, right between the eyes.

My next selection was from a musician Garvey had gotten me on to, a song I may have never heard had it not been for him – it was "Meeting Across the River", by Bruce Springsteen.

"Beautiful," Garvey smiled as those first desolate trumpet notes sounded.

There was some irony here, however. This song, a deep track on Springsteen's *Born To Run* album, originally struck me because it sounded so out of place on that record.

"I always thought this song had a more uniquely *noir* aspect to it than Springsteen's typical approach. It was more, um…what would the proper descriptive be? Elegant, maybe? It deviated from the emotional grit in the rest of this record, and yet it managed to sound even more desperate than he normally did somehow," I said.

"Agree," Garvey nodded as we listened to the conclusion together.

His turn now.

His next song was a live track, "Once Upon a Time in the West" from the Dire Straits' double live record *Alchemy*.

"This album made me a Dire Straits fan well before MTV turned them into big stars," Garvey gushed. "Listen to Knopfler's playing. Just *listen* to him! And with a guitar tone that's clean as a whistle."

I nodded my approval as it played. I understood why he might feel that way about it, and I appreciated the musicality, but I could never really care that much about it. Just not my cup of tea.

My next tune took us in a completely different direction. It was Califone's "Michigan Girls". Garvey would likely care for it about as much as I had cared for his previous selection, especially at this hour. I provided my perspective nonetheless.

"This is a mysterious, malevolent song that immediately charmed me the first time I heard it. Califone is a band that seems to go out of its way to unsettle the listener with all kinds of strange and unnecessary noise in their music, but they thankfully keep that stuff to a minimum here. They're a bit like Wilco that way, and I find it frustrating. Frustrating only because the basic musicianship is gifted and superior, such that it just makes the noise seem that much more pointless. If the band sucked, it would be expected and it wouldn't matter."

"I don't mind that about Wilco," Garvey said.

"I know you don't, but it pisses me off. There's no need for it. It can't be considered any form of artistic expression, even though I'm sure it is by somebody. It's just foolishness, the same type you see when you go to the art gallery and see a pile of actual garbage, like real actual refuse from someone's garbage can, and the artist is presenting it in some form of nouveau artistic medium. At best, this is capitalizing on the variance in our perceptive imaginations. At worst, he's taking advantage of the blind fucking wannabe sheep of our society."

Garvey began laughing and making bleating noises to knock me off my soapbox.

"It just frustrates me because it undermines how good the actual music could be," I continued.

"Maybe that *is* the music," he suggested.

"It's not. It can't be. Listen - here's the music, right here," I urged. We both fell silent as a line of lilting cello notes swelled from the sound dock serving as the crescendo of "Michigan Girls".

"Beautiful. See? *That's* the music," I said with a slanted smile, pressing pause and removing my iPod. Garvey looked at me with an adversarial smirk as he approached the dock with his next selection.

"Alright, whatcha got man?" I exhaled after swallowing the contents of my glass.

"Here's what I got," Garvey replied and pressed play dramatically.

"The fucking Go-Go's! Yes!" I said.

Another surprise. This was great.

"I love garage rock, and this song reflects my love for it. The Go-Go's are a garage band that got polished up. They wrote good, straight-up, simple rock songs with great grooves. This version of "We Got The Beat" was recorded before the radio hit version. It highlights the bass line more than the guitar, and gives it teeth the radio version lacks."

"Belinda Carlisle had a mysterious charm beyond her physical beauty," I offered.

"Indeed," Garvey agreed.

"I read an article somewhere wherein the guitar player…Jane Wiedlin is it? I think that's her name. Anyway, Jane was being interviewed by this magazine and she told this disgusting story about how her and another member of the band, I don't remember which one, but it certainly wasn't Belinda, used to go into truck stop bathrooms out of boredom when they were on the road and lick the corners of the floor on dares from each other.

She said they used to call each other The Super Suckers or something like that," I told Garvey.

His face soured. "What?!? Really?"

"Hey, you can't make this stuff up. I remember being so confused and mortified by that that I didn't bother to read the rest of the interview. I hate that I'm reminded of it every time I think of the Go-Go's. Curse you, Jane Wiedlin," I replied.

"Thank you for pulling me into your vortex of depravity," Garvey admonished.

"Come on, man. I'm just telling you what I read."

"I'll choose to pretend you didn't share that with me."

"Very well. My apologies for ruining the Go-Go's listening experience," I mocked. "Now get your player out of there. My turn."

"What time is it?" Garvey slurred.

"I dunno. No clocks in here. It's kinda like Vegas that way. Maybe they don't want us to know what time it is for some reason."

That didn't make any sense. Jessica didn't care if I knew what time it was.

I squinted down at my iPod.

"Ah. My old buddy again," I said.

"Nice," Garvey said quietly as he nodded along to David Bowie's "Starman". "What album is this from?"

"*Ziggy*," I responded. "So great."

Bowie's music had me completely transfixed for a lengthy period in my life. During that time, I didn't listen to much else. I learned all of Bowie's songs from *Ziggy Stardust and the Spiders from Mars* on guitar and when I played them, I would sing the words in an unapologetic Cockney accent. Because when you're a Canadian imitating a Brit, there are only two inflections used - Cockney, way over on the left, and proper posh, way over on the right. There's nothing in between.

"There's no denying the guy is a genius," Garvey said.

"Couldn't agree more. Rock's ultimate visionary. He was always ahead of the curve. He started out as simple David Jones, a frizzy-haired hippie folk musician, but he just kept growing and evolving. He was a great assimilator, and he saw the pop culture landscape with this incredible vision. Glam, soul, rock, dance - his only boundary was time, really."

"We have that in common," Garvey said. "Time is proving to be a major boundary to me right now. I have one more song in me and then I'm out."

"Alright, one more each," I conceded. "You're up."

"Springsteen again. Newer track."

"Is this "The Rising"?" I asked.

"Yep. Only Bruce can sing about 9/11 and avoid sounding cheesy. This is an anthem of courage that puts you right there, heading up a stairwell towards your doom, and somehow all you feel is inspired."

"Yeah, you're right." I agreed. "I actually like this song, because I believe it. That doesn't happen a lot for me with artists who might be closer to the ends of their careers than they are to the beginnings of them. Did I ever tell you that story about Springsteen and the Louvre?" I asked Garvey. I was sure I had.

He nodded his head affirmatively. "I think so, but it was a long time ago. And I'm sleepy. Sing it in the form of a lullaby."

"Whatever. The story goes that I had bumped into an old school buddy on the street a few years after we graduated," I started. "He had gone backpacking through Europe with another guy I knew from school. When they got to France, he told the other guy he had made one promise to his mom - that if he found himself in Paris during his travels, he had to go into the Louvre and take pictures. Or at the very least, get pictures of the outside of the building. It had been her childhood dream to experience it, but she never had, and likely would never find herself in the position to do so. He nor his friend particularly wanted to go to the Louvre, but they both agreed that they should."

"Good boys," Garvey muttered.

"So they're in the Louvre walking around, and my buddy's friend says, *'hey dude, look over there - that guy looks just like Bruce Springsteen'*. My buddy looks across the room and sees two men, the smaller one in fact looking a lot like The Boss. So they decide to get a bit closer.

"As they approach, it's evident that it is in fact Bruce Springsteen with what they assumed was a handler of some sort. They get close enough to him to try to make eye contact. He looks over at them and says, *'hey guys'*. He's super friendly. Then he notices the Canadian flag emblem sewn into my buddy's backpack and says, *'are you guys here from Canada?'* and they both smile and nod. So they end up talking about Europe and the challenges of being over there as a Westerner for like, ten or fifteen minutes. They said he was the nicest guy - completely engaging, and that he just seemed like another homesick traveller."

"That's awesome."

"So then, he asks them what they were doing that night."

"Okay…" Garvey responded, having perked up a bit.

"They told him nothing special, that they had no plans. So he asked them if they wanted to come to his show that night. He was doing smaller acoustic solo club dates across Europe, and he said he could put a couple of tickets aside if they wanted to go."

"That's fucking *crazy*," Garvey enthused.

"I know, right? So they say yes and provide their full names, which the handler writes down on a notepad. They shake hands with him and go on their way, completely freaked out."

"No kidding."

"So they get back to their hotel room at the end of the day, and look up the venue Bruce is playing at. It's way out of the way, a few hours from their hotel. They talk about the possibility of the tickets maybe not being there and how much it would suck if they went all that way for nothing, because the show was sold out. They had also planned to leave France early the next morning. So they consider not going."

"*Fools!!!*" Garvey yelled out in the old man voice.

"After a while they eventually agreed that they would kick themselves if they didn't go, forever wondering about what could have been. So they make the trip. When they show up at the will-call window, they're led around the building to the stage door and guided through the backstage area and then out front to their seats, which were right in front of the stage. The show was an acoustic gig, so there was a barstool and a microphone on stage, and that was it. At show time, out comes Bruce. He sits down on the stool with his guitar, looks down at them, winks and says, '*hey guys!*'"

Garvey's face reflects his wonderment.

"Can you fucking believe that?!?!" I said.

"That's why they call him The Boss," Garvey replied.

"Yep. The bad news is that my buddy's mom never did get her pictures of the Louvre."

CHAPTER 11

Now With Less Lightning

"That's okay, Canadian National Railway. I was ready to get up anyway," I mumbled under my breath as the train rocketed past our chalet, horn blaring its monotone warning a bit too early that morning.

My eyes opened and moved around the room as I familiarized myself with my surroundings. At least the sun was out. That always made me feel like I had a little bit more to give.

After a night like the one that had just passed, I always took a few moments to survey its stream of events. I sifted through the mental pictures while lying still on my back, reviewing the images before getting up and getting on with it. Not because it was preparation for anything. There wasn't any requirement for that at all. It was more just as curious reclamation.

I wondered about the state of my compatriot on the other side of the slatted doors that separated our sleeping quarters. The train had likely also forced his eyes open, but I couldn't hear him. I didn't know what time it was, but I liked that. I didn't want to be governed by time out here.

I made my way to the kitchen through the bathroom, so as not to wake Garvey should he still be sleeping. He wasn't. His face was mordant, and when his eyes found me that expression didn't change.

"*Toot toot!*" He mocked extra sardonically.

"No need for an alarm clock, I guess."

"It was time to get up anyway. We have work to do." Still sarcastic.

We mobilized our hungover carcasses towards the objective of making breakfast. Eggs, bacon, home fries, toast. I would handle the fried eggs and toast, while Garvey prepared his vile bacon. The thought of all that grease turned my stomach.

"Think the barbecue is fixed yet?" Garvey asked.

"We'll find out tonight," I answered, pouring myself a large glass of Five Alive. My head wasn't where I needed it to be yet. I placed my dependency on the citrus drink to help with that.

There was a knock on the door. A female other than Jessica was here to clean up this shambles.

"Would we just throw all of the empties in recycling, or would it make your life easier if we sorted everything?" Garvey asked our attendant, still in his underwear.

He had left his pullout bed unmade. His pillow case and accompanying paraphernalia were under cover. Not that it mattered to this young individual, out here on the border of British Columbia.

"Just throw them all in," she replied as she dropped a fresh batch of kindling beside the fireplace. "Did you guys want me to clear out all of the ash and debris here?" She pointed to the hearth.

"I guess we could have done that ourselves, but yes please," I responded. I didn't think she asked the question with any pointed purpose, but I couldn't be sure.

"We don't need her to make this place up, do we?" Garvey said to me in the kitchen. "I don't care if you don't."

"Nah. It's fine. Let's just clear away the garbage and we should be good."

Garvey reiterated this request to our host and she complied, shortly after doing away with the charred remains of last night's fires in and around the fireplace. We helped her replenish the pile of wood with what we would burn after dark later that night, and expressed our thanks for her services as she drove her little John Deere firewood delivery tractor away.

"Oh, wait!" Garvey yelled to her.

She cut the engine and lifted her eyebrows in anticipation of his request.

"We had some trouble with the barbecue last night. Would you know if it's working now?" he asked.

"Yeah, it works. Someone looked at it this morning. Good to go," she responded politely before driving away.

Garvey came back into the kitchen.

"I wonder if that was a congenial way of saying '*learn how to work a barbecue, dickhead*'," he deadpanned.

"It's possible that whoever used it before us didn't turn off the propane, and we were turning it the wrong way," I surmised. Garvey snickered at the potential for our ineptitude.

"They hate us here already," he concluded.

After the breakfast dishes were cleared away, and after we discussed in detail several of the things we had done in our youth for which we should have gone to jail, we set about our task of continuing to reach into the beauty of our songs with the intention of smearing it all over ourselves once again.

It was probably noon by now. Welcomed sunshine beamed down into our chalet through the skylights, outlasting lonely clouds as they floated by.

"So when do you want to do the mushrooms?" Garvey asked with a grin.

"Fuck, man. I'm still nervous about that for some reason."

"Why? It's completely organic. What are you nervous about?"

"What if I freak out and do something crazy?"

"Like what, laugh until you piss your pants?" Garvey reasoned. "Nothing freaky will happen. It's not like acid or anything."

He was right, of course. I had never taken acid. I was apprehensive about anything beyond the standard narcotic fare. Although I suppose for some, acid had been standard in younger years. But not for me, man. None of that stuff was. At sixteen, I had seen a video in my physical education class where some reprobate took angel dust, elected to pull every one of his teeth out with a pair of pliers, and then proceeded to go on a destructive rampage before being detained by multiple police officers. Dude snapped a pair of five hundred pound test handcuffs during this detainment. No thanks.

I always fear the worst in any situation. That's how I deal with things. With mushrooms, my mind initially fails to recognize their subtlety when compared with acid, PCP, or peyote in the face of a potential loss of self-control. They're all hallucinogens, and thus each one of these drugs carried equal opportunity to compel me to remove my teeth with pliers. That's the logic I use in assessment.

"It would be terrible if you didn't do them and I did mine by myself. That would really suck," Garvey appealed.

Peer pressure still impacted me, even in my forties. Some things never change.

"Let's have a look at them," I said.

I already knew I was going to go ahead with it. So did Garvey.

He produced a small ceramic container that resembled a mushroom, with cutesy facial features painted onto it as you might find in your grandmother's kitchen.

"Drug users are so acerbically clever," I commented as he removed the lid. Inside were what looked like two cylindrical earplugs.

"Isn't this great? You don't have to take them in those small pieces that get lodged in your teeth anymore. One easily swallowed pellet now," Garvey enthused.

"The marvels of science and progress," I responded, still somewhat irrationally nervous.

I think my primary concern was really the potential to lose control over what we were doing here, to jeopardize what I hoped to get out of it somehow.

"So when are we doing these little numbers? I would suggest we take them on an empty stomach." Garvey was so bloody meticulous with his hallucinogens.

"Whenever you're ready, pal," I responded. "I'm with you."

"*Yay!*" Garvey exclaimed in the voice. "Ah, I knew you would. Let's wait a couple of hours and pop 'em then."

"Alright," I responded.

Garvey opened a beer and took his position in his listening chair.

"Alright, motherfucker. Play me a song."

I walked past the acoustic guitars that we hadn't played the night before, and over to the table where I had left my iPod. I was pleased with the timing of my next song, as I had wanted for Garvey to really pay attention to the sonic aspects involved. We would be off to a roaring start. This was one of my favourite heavy metal anthems, "Balls to the Wall" by German band Accept.

"You may have heard this song before, but I want you to really listen to the guitar tracks here. They crunch with a perfection like I haven't heard in any other recording," I instructed. I was a nerd with this stuff.

The song's main riff poured from the sound dock. I felt its power in my chest.

"Yeah," Garvey said. "It's definitely textbook. I love that tone."

As a guitar player with a fanatical appreciation for tone, I knew Garvey would hear this with an unbiased ear. During the guitar solo, he noted my enthusiasm and gauged my fondness of this music with a knowing smile. It was so great to have him here, to share this stuff with him.

"You're up, pally," I resigned.

"This song is called "Tired of Being Alone". It's Al Green," Garvey told me.

"Soul," I said, sitting back in my chair.

"Memphis soul, at its absolute zenith. It gets no better than this. This is why I hear horns in my head when I imagine how guitar parts should sound."

There was no question that this music was soothing. It paired well with the sunshine pouring in through the windows. I considered the application of this music in my own life. It would never mean as much to me as it did to Garvey, but I did enjoy it.

The song was short, and Garvey ran over to hit the pause button. He forewent pause, instead just yanking his iPod out of the system altogether.

"Almost showed my next card there."

"It's still early yet," I reminded.

I was more inclined now to think that there would be a time towards the end of this program where we would just let the songs run, distracted by a combination of the bottle and philosophical bullshitting. I readied my next song, which ran completely counter to my previous selection. I unleashed a hypnotic, slightly distorted acoustic guitar line upon hitting the play button.

"Who's this?" Garvey perked up.

"It's a guy named Devendra Banhart. The song is called "A Sight to Behold"," I said.

"I like this. I like this a lot."

I had to admit I did enjoy when Garvey took a particular liking to one of my selections.

"It's haunting. It's so lo-fi and simple that I almost feel like this individual is actually trying to communicate with me. Apparently this song and the remainder of this record were recorded in his living room," I said.

"This is really unique. I'll have to look it up."

"What's next?" I asked.

Garvey consulted his playlist as I punched out. "Another newer tune. Jack White."

"Lazaretto!" I yelled out.

"Nope. Older newer."

It was hard to keep track of Jack White's many musical exploits these days.

"This is "Love Interruption"," Garvey stated. "I needed something current on this list. Jack White puts a fresh spin on country blues, and he created a minimalist gem here."

"I like this, especially that electric piano. And his lyrics are always intense and interesting. But I prefer his more fast-paced stuff. For a while he was coming out blazing with that first single, like "Blue Orchid". Then I would buy the record and the rest of it sounded like some peculiar inside joke that I didn't get," I said.

"Eh?"

"You know. Like "My Doorbell", from The White Stripes' *Get Behind Me Satan*," I explained. "I wanted an album of just "Blue Orchids", and it was disappointing when no other song on the record even resembled it. Kinda like Lenny Kravitz. He used to do a similar thing."

"What do you mean?"

"The leadoff single for the record was always a balls-out rocker, like "Are You Gonna Go My Way", "Always on the Run", or "Rock and Roll is Dead". But then you'd find out the rest of the album was all ballads after buying it," I clarified.

"That's artistry," Garvey said mockingly.

"That's bullshit," I laughed. "At least it only took me three albums to get wise to it."

I pressed play on my next song, "Life in a Northern Town" by Dream Academy, before going into the kitchen to open a bottle of vino.

Crap. Last bottle.

"We're going to need more supplies, frère," I noted.

"They sell booze at that little store near the office. We'll head down there later and get some chips and stuff too," he said, staring at the sound dock. "Great song."

"Do you remember this?" I asked, less in the form of a question than an invitation to discuss the track.

"Yeah, the golden age of *Friday Night Videos*. This and "Come On Eileen"," Garvey said.

"Exactly," I agreed.

"As a kid, I looked for identification cues inside this song based on the title and the overall gloominess of it. It wasn't necessarily my thing at the time, but I was always doing that with music as a teenager, regardless of genre - anything that seemed to have the slightest potential for connectivity was romanticized. I bent the purposes of these songs for my own needs. Everything I listened to had to have a personal, relatable meaning. Some form of identifiable message."

"So greedy," Garvey joked.

"It was. But I think all music lovers are inherently greedy and selfish, because the love for music is rooted in vanity. Music's like a mirror we hold up in front of ourselves with the intention of looking at our insides, even more so when we're younger and don't have any of the answers yet."

"How many answers have you got so far?" Garvey asked.

"More than I did back then. Don't have them all yet though."

"Will you ever?"

Pause.

"I think I'm getting closer."

I felt like the answer could not have been *yes* at that point, but I couldn't bring myself to respond in the negative. Songs like "Life in a Northern Town" were my crutches, my representative emblems as a confused kid. I saw these songs as being there solely for me to invest my loneliness into. I wanted them to be artistic representations of my emotional burdens, so that I might be relieved of them in some romantic, dramatic way. Our differences were so apparent in that way, Garvey and I. The peace in his playlist betrayed that fact. It was a fact I was reminded of every time he hit play.

I punched out, and Garvey punched in. His next song was warm and familiar.

""Do It Again", Steely Dan. Love this," I said.

"Is this the first time we both have different songs from the same album?" Garvey inquired.

"I think so, yeah. Unless you had something from *Born To Run* earlier. Did you play "Jungleland" yesterday? I think you did."

"Yeah, you're right. I did. Anyway, this whole first Steely Dan record is great. Steely Dan is a band for every context. This album was in the milk crates full of LPs that Uncle Barry gave me," Garvey told me.

Those were the same milk crates that inspired The Record Game.

"I wish we could play The Record Game right now," I said. "Let's make a point of doing that some time."

"Do you think it would be the same?"

Another pause.

"No," I dismissed. "We could never get that lightning back in the bottle."

This consideration depressed me a little more than it should have.

The lightning from yesterdays was gone. But at least the music was still here in commemoration.

The little store at Castle Mountain Chalets wasn't really like a store. It was more like a collection of things off to the side of the check-in area, things you may have brought with you and ran out of, or had intended to bring and forgot. It reminded me of the tiny small town confectionaries of my youth, little converted homes with white makeshift Pure Spring cream soda signs hanging out front and run by affable elderly men and their wives. This one was run by a much younger person, another of Jessica's Australian cohorts.

"Any bear sightings yet today?" I asked the young kid as I plunked a few bottles down on the counter.

"Yep. Every day. People get eaten alive out here man, it's crazy," he responded in an Aussie accent.

"You're screwing with us," Garvey said.

"Yeah, of course. It doesn't happen *every* day."

I smirked as he handed me my change. "Thanks for the heads up."

"Enjoy your stay," he enthused.

Garvey and I left the confectionary and made the fifty foot walk back to our chalet, now fortified with two bags of Ruffles sour cream and onion potato chips, one bag of Oreo cookies, two Kit Kat chocolate bars, and a few bottles of red and white wine. No bears in sight.

"Here's a little something snappy for you," I said as I pressed play back inside the chalet. "My next song is called "This Head I Hold" by Electric Guest."

"Who the fuck is *this*?!" Garvey asked.

"Electric Guest," I repeated. "It's manufactured pop masquerading as R&B in a tongue-in-cheek kinda way. A guilty pleasure. I couldn't stop listening to this when I first heard it, it's so bloody catchy. Listen to those little snare drum snaps. It's fake, but it's so irresistible. I can't help myself."

"Man, this is weird. And *good*. It's got that classic R&B swing, y'know?"

"Right? I love it," I said.

"Where did you hear this?"

"Satellite radio. The same place I heard Foster The People, MGMT, and Oregon Bike Trails. It's like musical Hubba Bubba. Sugary, disposable, but tasty to chew on for a little while."

Garvey reached for his iPod after the song ended.

"Let's go back the other way for a minute," Garvey said as he pressed play.

"Ah, well done sir. The Black Crowes," I responded. The song was "Thorn in my Pride".

"That's three times now. At least three times, I think."

"What's that?"

"That our lists have contained different songs from the same record," I answered.

"Likely won't be the last time," Garvey expressed. "This song, in my opinion, is the best song off of the best record ever made by the most underrated band of the past thirty years. The guitar tones come straight from heaven, and the interplay between the instruments is absolutely beautiful."

Another bold statement. But this was the place to make those proclamations. We could say anything we wanted to say here, and I would be the last guy to dissuade such decrees. This was what I wanted.

I consulted my iPod for my next selection. I liked the intrigue of not knowing what would come next. Anything could come out of the iPod, and it kept things interesting. My next selection had a similarly easy vibe as the last song, however. It was Foreigner's "Waiting For A Girl Like You".

"The sleepy keyboard swells that introduce this song have this uncanny ability to put me right back into 1981. Whenever I hear them coming it's almost like I'm back there, with very vivid memories of my childhood surroundings - the people, the streets, all the details. Everything. This song is like a time machine in that sense. Not too many other songs can do that for me, and that's why this song made my playlist. It's powerful that way," I explained.

"Nostalgia in general is a powerful concept, my friend."

"Tell me about it," I responded. "Aside from that, this whole record is actually pretty good."

"What's this on again?"

"*4. Foreigner 4*," I specified.

"With "Urgent", right?"

"Yes, that big sax solo. Great song. But the whole album flows nicely, from "Night Life" and "Juke Box Hero" through the deeper cuts like "Girl on the Moon". It sounds like an album that was recorded in 1981, and I like that," I said.

"Speaking of which, here's something from the early 80s you might dig," Garvey segued. "Springsteen's "The River"."

"I believe The Boss is currently holding the MVP designation for most number of tracks played so far," I observed.

"He deserves it. His stuff is upper echelon," Garvey responded. "Early Springsteen records were hopeful. They were about the potential for being able to escape your circumstances. On the three records that followed *Born to Run*, the characters in his songs realized that they actually couldn't outrun their circumstances, and hope flickered. I think *The River* is probably the single best example of that."

As I listened, my mind reached back to a time in early 2000 when I visited Garvey in Memphis. During this time he had bought us tickets to see Springsteen at a venue called The Pyramid. It stood out in my mind as being one of the most enjoyable rock shows I'd ever seen.

There was no opener, because Bruce played for three or four hours. When the lights went down, the E Street Band members emerged from the back of the stage one by one, each garnering massive amounts of adulation from the crowd. The cheers would grow progressively louder and louder as each member appeared from the darkness - Garry Tallent, then Roy Bittan. Then Nils Lofgren. Max Weinberg. Patti Scialfa. And then the big man, Clarence Clemons. People went nuts.

And you know who was next. When The Boss came out, the place absolutely exploded. The band went right into their first song, which was unfamiliar to me, but it didn't matter because the vibe was like nothing I'd ever witnessed up to that point. I do remember the second song, as it's a Springsteen favourite of mine - "Prove It All Night". "The River" got played that night too, as did "Meeting Across The River" and "Jungleland". The highlight of the show, among many, was the performance of "Born to Run" during the first encore. It was an incredible experience I'll never forget.

I felt like something of a convert after that show. I felt like I'd been lucky enough to see a true rock and roll deity in a genuine place of musical worship. It was as though I had been properly sorted out as a fan of rock music after that. And I had the guy who was currently sitting across from me to thank for it.

CHAPTER 12

One Small Step

The sun's position in the sky suggested that morning was gone, but that there were still a number of hours after noon available for our use. Keeping my mind off of them wouldn't help them to lapse any more slowly.

My next selection was "All The Things I Wasn't" by Canadian group The Grapes of Wrath. It was a bit of late 80s folk-rock introspection, succinct and quietly sure of itself. It was a simple amalgam of acoustic guitar melody, sombre string section and a brief piano line that I could never resist. Here at the chalet, we weren't so far from where the band got its start in Kelowna, British Columbia. Regardless of geography, I had always felt a connection to this group. Another of their songs, "Backward Town", could have also made my playlist.

"If you didn't know this was Canadian, would it sound Canadian to you?" I asked Garvey, who was likely the proudest Canuck of all my friends. He had a small Canadian flag tattooed on his right shoulder.

"You mean does it have a Canadian *sound*?"

"I guess so, yeah."

"I don't think *this* song does in particular. For me, it has more of a broader, REM-meets-Simon-and-Garfunkel melancholic vibe. But a lot of their other songs did sound Canadian to me," Garvey said.

"Yeah, I think you're right," I agreed. "Their other stuff had that certain Canuck amiability, no? It sounds like an aural smile, and it seemed to fit right in with the other Canadian bands of that time. These bands didn't necessarily sound the same, but they seemed to be unified by that common thread - The Spirit of the West, The Barenaked Ladies, The Rheostatics, Skydiggers...," I trailed off.

"Yep," Garvey agreed.

"And The Pursuit of Happiness," I blurted out. "Their name underscores the entire idea. That's a Canadian band name if ever there was one."

I continued. "You're up. Now be a good patriot and put something Canadian on."

"I already did."

"What was it?"

"The Band."

"Ah. Not quite the same," I said.

"What do you want, fucking Luba? Parachute Club?"

"I was thinking more Martha and the Muffins. Come on. "Echo Beach" is on your playlist, isn't it?" I asked.

"It is not. The Band is. As is Neil Young," Garvey reminded.

"I don't necessarily think of Neil Young as Canadian. His music doesn't have that Canadian vibe. In my mind, he's Canadian in the same way that Jim Carrey or Lorne Michaels are. He's an American Canadian," I reasoned. This comment would likely raise Garvey's ire.

"And Joni Mitchell?" he responded.

"Yes, and Joni Mitchell. Same. Joni's more Laurel Canyon than Saskatchewan."

There was the ire. It came in the form of Charles Bronson cut-eye.

"Time for you to be quiet and listen to this."

"What is it?" I asked with mock sheepishness.

"Wilco. The song is "I Am Trying to Break Your Heart"."

"So no Canadian content then?"

Garvey ignored me and pressed play, then returned to his chair.

"I love the way Jeff Tweedy isn't afraid to experiment with noise. I know you don't, based on our conversation yesterday. I'll agree with you, ninety-nine percent of the artists that do it alienate me. But when Wilco does it, it intrigues me. And the lyrics make Gord Downie's seem straightforward."

I listened intently as the song played, then offered my two cents.

"You know I'm not a proponent of the use of noise at all. Like I said yesterday, I think it's annoying and pointless. But I can deal with this - it doesn't seem as though it's included with the intention of indifference here. It's interwoven with the main instruments and seems meaningful as a component of the song. Except maybe those atonal piano notes. I don't see the point of those," I said.

The jauntiness of the song's end segment was playing now.

"And the end. This is my point. Just end the goddamn song already," I continued. This stuff irritated me.

Garvey laughed. "You should have been a record executive in the 70s, when they carved every song down to three minutes and five seconds."

"That was just to get it on AM radio. I don't really give a fuck about the radio."

"You only give a fuck about sucking the artistry out of artists," Garvey mocked.

"If it was artistry, it wouldn't be pointless."

"To each his own, pal."

"No judgment," I smirked after Wilco's last bit of meaningless buzzing finally subsided.

"Your turn, Judge Jensen," Garvey ridiculed.

"I can assure you there will be none of that nonsense in my next selection, even before I look at it," I advised, hoping it was not a Califone song.

I looked down at the iPod.

Whew. Far from it.

"Give me the rundown," Garvey huffed. He was all business now.

"Okay, this is a cover song," I said over the crowd noise and brooding introductory piano notes of this live recording. "A cover of a terrible Black Sabbath deep cut from their second worst Ozzy-era record, *Technical Ecstasy*. The song is called "It's Alright". This song is on Guns N' Roses' live record, and Axl plays it as a type of introductory lead-in to "November Rain". I hadn't heard it before, but when I did I knew it wasn't a Guns song. So I looked it up in the liner notes and saw that it was written by Bill Ward. I figured this would likely be the same Bill Ward of Black Sabbath fame. This cover was from sometime in the mid-90s, so without the luxury of the all-knowing internet, I went down to Sam the Record Man on Yonge Street and went through Sabbath's records looking for it."

"You didn't know it was a Black Sabbath song, and you call yourself a heavy metal fan?" Garvey was still trying to wind me up.

"I'm disappointed in you, Garvey. Clearly you don't read my books," I said.

"Anyway, so I find this song on Sabbath's *Technical Ecstasy*, and I buy the CD figuring it's going to be super good. And it ain't."

"It's not good?" Garvey questioned.

"It's really bad, in fact. It's flat and toothless and overproduced. Poor Billy even sings the track, unconvincingly. I was disappointed and kind of astonished at the same time. Except with the lyrics. The lyrics are fantastic. And this is why I think Axl plucked this rough diamond out of obscurity. He gravitated to the lyrics, saw potential in the song, and through his tortured affect, produced something incredible. This song is an example of Axl's musical genius."

This comment would likely also draw ire from Garvey. And we hadn't even really started drinking yet.

"Interesting observation," he responded smugly.

"Axl was like King Midas back then. He took songs like this one, as well as others that were already quality songs and made them even better."

"Such as?"

"Such as "Live and Let Die"."

"Be careful there. You're bordering on sacrilege," Garvey said.

"One of my favourite rock and roll stories has to do with Sir Paul himself and this song," I went on. "Macca took his daughter Stella to a Guns N' Roses concert in the early 90s at her insistence."

"Right," Garvey said.

"So they're standing there watching the show, and his daughter is loving it. Halfway through the set, the band plays "Live and Let Die". Paul looks at his daughter and says in her ear, '*you know, your dad wrote this song*'. And she looks back at him and responds, '*whatever, Dad*'."

Garvey snorted. "I like that."

"It's Alright" concluded and leaked into the beginning of my next selection.

Dang.

I had committed my first foul of the proceedings. However, I recognized that it was an artist double-play, so it kinda contributed to my point.

"Mind if I let this play? It emphasizes the point I was making," I requested.

"Be my guest," Garvey allowed.

The next song was a bootleg of Guns N' Roses doing a loose, jammy acoustic version of "Jumpin' Jack Flash" before their world domination period, maybe 1986. It sounded like it had been recorded inside a pop can.

"Listen to how Axl adds a new vocal melody in the chorus instead of just singing what's already there. He takes a great song to a new level. And he does it twice, with *two* new melodies, both of which are killer. It's exciting stuff," I emphasized. "Listen to this young kid's voice. You can hear the power and the promise in it."

Garvey was nonplussed. "You think he's a musical genius?"

I was prepared to make a bold statement of my own at this point.

"I will go on record as saying that I do. He has that vision, he has talent, and he has that aspect of imbalance that sets him apart. I think he's recognized for it by people who pay attention and understand. But I think a lot of other people don't pay attention because of all of the eccentricity that obscures the evidence of his vision. The sad thing is that he won't ever be widely recognized for it until he dies. And if he were to die earlier than expected, he would be celebrated as a martyr. Particularly if he died by his own hand, like Kurt Cobain did."

Garvey raised his eyebrows.

"I can guarantee you that had Axl shot himself in the head in 1992 it would be his name in the lyrics that all those people subsequently wrote, the ones that drop Cobain's name alongside John Lennon's and all of our other pop-mythologized fallen heroes," I vowed.

"Think so?" Garvey asked.

"I'm sure of it. People love their posthumous heroes so desperately. I hate when you hear Cobain's name in a lyric suggesting an equality with Lennon. It's lazy and careless. I respectfully give the guy credit as an artist, but that's where it ends for me. The canon of his work doesn't come close to measuring up to Lennon's."

"Were you ever a Nirvana fan?"

"No, not really. I appreciated them from a distance, and I got what they were doing and why. The time was definitely right for them to emerge, the same way punk did in rising up against the schmaltz of 70s stadium rock. But Nirvana did it with a menace that was much more intense and real. I did admire that Nirvana's enmity was so refined and sharp, because it *was* real. It wasn't just a gimmick to sell records. The clearest representation of this idea, the one that always resonated with me, was that line from "Heart Shaped Box" that went, '*I wish that I could eat your cancer when you turn black*'. Y'know, people had been trying to achieve that degree of disturbance for years! Bands like Venom tried so hard to disturb people with record after record of spooky Black Metal, but it was more or less received as a cartoon. With that one line, Nirvana delivered more malevolence than Venom or any of those other bands could have ever hoped to. Just with that one line."

"Would you write a lyric linking John Lennon to Axl Rose?" Garvey posed. It was a fair question.

"No. Never."

"I'm not sold on the whole *Axl-is-a-genius* thing. Has he released an album since *Chinese Democracy*?" Garvey lamented.

"No."

"He's been touring on that thing for like five years now, hasn't he?"

"I'm sure they have another album or two in the can," I reasoned.

While Garvey and I talked, a third song from my playlist had already begun to play. It was also Guns N' Roses, but the song was "There Was a Time" from *Chinese Democracy*. It was timely, so I made no attempt to stop it from playing.

"Your song maintenance is quite sloppy, sir" Garvey chastised. "Who is this?"

"Do you like it?"

"Yeah, it's not bad. Who is it?"

"Your buddy Axl. It's from *Chinese Democracy*."

"Bah," Garvey said, his face shrivelling.

"See? You liked it until I told you who it was!" I shrieked.

Garvey listened more intently. "This ain't the Axl of old. His voice sounds thin."

"I'll give you that. But he can still sing notes in almost six octaves, and he sings the highest one in this song - an F1. And apparently he has a lower baritone than Barry White. He sang a B flat 6 in "Ain't It Fun"".

"That's bullshit," Garvey contested. "You're making this up."

"No, it's not bullshit. I'm not messing with you, it's true. His vocals were measured using scientific pitch notation. Axl can actually reach higher notes than Beyoncé and Mariah Carey. He has the widest vocal range in popular music," I said as Axl's voice soared through the vocal outro of "There Was a Time." The song ended, and I looked at Garvey.

"Well?" I asked.

"I like it," he acquiesced.

I saluted his admission. "One small step for Garvey, one large step for mankind."

⋆

"This is a great Ryan Adams tune from a great Ryan Adams record," I said in response to Garvey's next selection, "Come Pick Me Up". "It's so snotty, and yet also so heartfelt. Nobody does that like Adams."

"I think this is *the* perfect Ryan Adams song because yes, it's beautiful and biting at the same time. A little country, a little folk, and a little punk," Garvey added.

"The first time I heard this song was early one afternoon in a honky-tonk on Lower Broad in Nashville, performed by an amazing singer. What I love about Nashville is that there are musicians everywhere, and the bar has been raised so high that everyone has to be incredibly talented. Even the panhandlers sitting on the sidewalks are fantastic singers. You just wanna ask them, *'man, what the hell happened to you?!?'*"

"But you know what happened to them," Garvey said.

"It was clear after having been there for a weekend, yes," I responded. "The law of natural selection happened to them. There isn't enough room for everyone who gets off the Greyhound with aspirations of fame. Not to mention the fact that everyone in Nashville will tell you that afternoon drinking is a time-honoured tradition. I'm sure that's a slippery slope for some folks."

"Indeed," Garvey recognized.

I continued on. "So the first time I was in Nashville, some friends and I were walking by this bar and we could hear a girl singing from outside. After hearing her voice, we had to go in for a drink and hear more. She blew us away when she played "Come Pick Me Up". She just had such a great singing voice. My friends and I were stunned. We ended up blowing off our dinner reservations to hang out at this bar all night. We ended up becoming friends with her over the weekend, and I mailed her my copy of

Ryan Adams' *Gold* when I got home. She had never heard *Gold*, and I told her that she really needed to," I told Garvey.

"Ever the gentleman," he said.

"That first afternoon after she played "Come Pick Me Up", I was talking with one of the locals about Ryan Adams. I guess they weren't really familiar with who he was as much as just with the song itself. I was telling the story about how Adams kicked a concertgoer out of one of his shows in the middle of a gig."

"Yeah?" Garvey said.

"The story was that Ryan Adams is up there playing, and some wiseass in the crowd keeps shouting out "*Summer of '69*" between songs trying to be funny. So Adams finally has enough of it. He reaches into his pocket, pulls out thirty bucks and throws it at the guy, and shouts '*get the fuck out of here!*'"

Garvey laughed.

"So I'm telling this story to this guy in Nashville now, expecting him to laugh or say '*whoa*', or something, right?"

"Yeah."

"And the guy squints and says to me, '*why didn't he just play the song? It's one of his biggest hits.*' And I pause. Then I say, '*Ryan Adams…?*' and he says, '*oh - I thought we were talking about Bryan Adams*'."

Garvey shook his head. "Poor Ryan Adams," he said. "He does do a Bryan Adams tune live now though. He does "Run To You"."

"I guess he just got worn down after years of drunken assholes yelling out Bryan Adams hits from the crowd."

"Yep. If you can't beat 'em, join 'em."

"I was reading the other day that Bryan Adams admitted that "Summer of '69" is actually about the sexual position, and not a reference to the actual summer of 1969."

"What did you think it was about?"

"When I was a kid in 1984, I thought the summer of 1969, I guess," I responded. "Adams' co-writer Jim Vallance was telling everyone it was, and I think Adams was too until just recently."

"Really?"

"Yeah. Apparently the song was initially called "Best Days of My Life", and the lyric '*summer of '69*' only appeared once in one of the verses. But they went through and replaced most of the '*best days of my life*' lines with '*summer of '69*' and changed the title of the song at Adams' request."

"I had an idea of that. Mostly because Adams sings '*me and my baby in a 69*' in that ad-lib at the end of the song," Garvey said.

"Yeah. It's clever because when he sings it, it almost sounds like he's just adding emphasis to the word *sixty*."

"The same way some Italians do," Garvey jumped in.

"Yeah, exactly," I laughed. "*A large a-pizza a-pie-a!*"

"Apparently Adams sang that line on the demo version before the song got changed around. Vallance thought he was just screwing around and wouldn't include it in the finished version, but Adams wanted it in and so it ended up in the final mix."

"Ah, the travails of the rock star," Garvey said as he punched out. "Alright, whaddaya got next?"

"Something with which to terrify and titillate you," I answered, only somewhat joking. I had Human League's "(Keep Feeling) Fascination".

"Holy fuck, are you kidding me?!?" Garvey responded. "What is this doing on your playlist?"

"I've always had a bizarre preoccupation with this keyboard riff. Listen to it. It's deranged and terrifying. And I don't even know that it's intentional. There's something vicious and twisted and unsettling about the way it sounds, don't you think?" I asked. I loved the weirdness of this song.

"What if that menacing synth riff was horns?" Garvey asked.

"Wouldn't be the same for me. It might still be a decent song, but not at all the same."

"Weird," Garvey expressed as he reached for his iPod after the song ended.

"Here's another Al Green song. You know this one."

"Yep. "Love and Happiness"," I replied after it started.

"It's a great song. And then when the horn-led breakdown happens, then it's a *fucking* great song," Garvey exalted.

I could see familiar patterns developing now after hearing all of these songs, and seeing inside my friend's musical DNA. I felt like I was unlocking a secret template. The drinks had already started flowing for the day, but soon it would be time to take the mushrooms. I wondered what kind of a role they would play as we continued to work through our playlists. It may have been interesting to listen to my next song under their sway.

"Ever heard this one?" I asked as I pressed play.

"Nope. Who's this?"

"Do you like it?"

"Just tell me who it is."

"Axl Rose," I said. I was lying.

"Come on!"

"I'm kidding. It's called "Opened Once", by Jeff Buckley."

I don't think any other song has affected me so immediately upon the first listen. This was a special song. It grabbed me by the shirt the very first time.

"Very atmospheric," Garvey intoned.

We both sat quietly, listening to this song as if in some form of commemoration, until its sudden but not jarring ending. I loved that the ending flouted expected structure; the end happens before I felt like it should. It almost seemed as though there was something more to be conveyed in this song, but the end prevents it - all of a sudden there wouldn't be any more. I always wanted this song to continue to play a little longer every time it ended. Garvey and I were silent for a moment after its conclusion, in reverence. And then, just like that, the moment faded into the ether. Gone.

"You're up," I said as I passed Garvey's listening post on my way to the kitchen for a refill.

"What have we got here…," Garvey's lips barely moved as he studied his playlist.

"Ah!" He smiled and punched in.

"I love Velvet Underground and I love Lou Reed. Simple, pretty songs about dark, ugly things," Garvey said about his song, "Oh! Sweet Nothing".

"I don't know a lot about Lou Reed and I know even less about Velvet Underground, but I do know that Reed was pretty friendly with David Bowie," I said. "Bowie often did little tributes to his idols, in the way that "Queen Bitch" was a shout-out to Velvet Underground."

"Right," Garvey said.

"Do you think that there's a connection between Bowie's song "Oh! You Pretty Things" from *Hunky Dory*, and Velvet Underground's "Oh! Sweet Nothing" by way of that 'Oh!' at the beginning at both of them?"

"Probably," Garvey supposed. "Not sure."

"I should get into Velvet Underground. I always tend to forget about them for some reason."

"*Blaspheme!*" Garvey shouted in that stupid voice. I wasn't expecting it and spit up some of my drink in response. I looked down to see it on my shirt.

"You clown," I said, laughing. "Get your goddamn iPod out of there."

I walked up to the sound dock and *ka-chiked* with exaggerated authority.

"What's the name of this song?"

"It's called "My Old Man" from *Blue*. I could have put a lot of different Joni Mitchell songs on this playlist, but what's special about this one is coming up in a minute. Hang on," I urged.

We sat silent, me nodding slightly as if I could somehow fast-forward the song with my head.

"Okay, here. Listen to this chord change right here," I enthused.

As the song went into its bridge, the chord change sent a small surge through me as I stared at Garvey for his approval. The change was that close to being magic.

"Did you hear that? Do you know what I mean? The chord change is unique and kinda takes you by surprise. It stirs something. Did you get that?" I asked.

All of a sudden I was like that yappy little dog Chester from *Bugs Bunny*, to Garvey's gruff Spike. Clearly there was little need for mushrooms.

"No, I didn't really get that," he said.

"Really? Bah."

Such was the push and pull of our musical brotherhood. It would be unreasonable for us to experience the same sensations all the time, I suppose. Illegitimate.

Garvey's next selection was familiar to me. A friend had provided me with a copy of the album years ago. It was The Black Keys' "I Got Mine". Great pick. I needed to dust off that record.

"This was at the point in The Black Keys' career when their rawness was just the right amount of refined. That greasy groove was still intact. I have no idea how Dan Auerbach plays this and sings over it while keeping such great time," Garvey commented.

I nodded in recognition.

"It's interesting to watch people play who have that ability. I could never do it." Hell, I had a hard time playing Bowie's "The Man Who Sold the World" and singing it at the same time.

My next song sent Garvey outside, the same way a band's new material sends audience members fleeing for pee breaks at live shows.

"This is pure heavy metal might," I said sarcastically through my teeth at Garvey, who was inhaling something on the other side of the front door. The song was Judas Priest's "Riding on the Wind", a near-perfect heavy metal representation.

"You hate it that much, eh?" I yelled over to him.

"No, it just sounds better out here," he smiled. "The acoustics are better."

He came in just before it was over and sat down in his chair.

"I used to listen to heavy metal as a kid," Garvey shared.

"Come on," I said in disbelief. I had no idea after all this time.

"No, I did. Seriously. I used to go into my bedroom on the second floor, dress up, and put on Judas Priest's *Defenders of the Faith*. I have a terrible story about it, as a matter of fact."

"Really? What do you mean *dress up*? You gotta tell me this story."

"I used to put on these ski goggles and dress up in other stuff that I thought looked vaguely rock and roll, and I would pretend I was playing the songs live. I had a hockey stick that I propped up as a mic stand, and I used a tennis racket for a guitar. Standard stuff. I fully rocked out to Ratt and Judas Priest in front of my bedroom window, and I left the curtains open so I could see myself in the reflection," Garvey confessed.

"Did your bedroom back on to like, a field or something? You weren't worried about anybody looking in at you?" I asked.

"No, it faced out into the street. That's the bad news. One night during one of my performances I could hear something outside between songs. I looked down, and there was a group of my friends standing there in front of my house cheering."

"Oh Christ," I gasped. "What did you do?"

"I pretended like I knew they were there and I just kept going, trying to be cool about it. Then I noticed that there were some girls mixed in to the group. Girls I liked."

"Ouch. And who perhaps may have liked you back, until they witnessed your concert with the goggles and the tennis racket?"

"Yes."

I was laughing like a hyena at the thought of this. "Oh, man. That's fucking terrible." I sputtered. "So is your next song by Ratt then?"

"No it's not, Beavis. Get a hold of yourself." I was almost choking.

Garvey removed my iPod from the sound dock with a little extra *ka-chik*, and inserted his and pressed play. It wasn't Ratt, nor was it anything I expected.

"Come on! Public Enemy?" I asked. The surprise abruptly ended my laughing fit.

"That's right. "Fight the Power"," Garvey confirmed.

"Wow. Great pick. Please explain."

"Just listen to those lyrics. *'Elvis was a hero to some but he didn't mean shit to me'*. This is powerful stuff. There's poetry, grooves, revolutionary arrangements. I like very little hip hop or rap, but I really like this."

"I got into this at school a bit too. I liked the aggression, and I was just as interested in the bizarre polarization of Chuck D and Flavor Flav. I could never figure out what the deal was with Terminator X. He was the guy who just stood in the back and ruined styluses, right?" I asked.

"Yeah. I didn't know much about the band, really."

"It was interesting when they did their thing with Anthrax," I suggested. "I was excited by that as a metal fan. I liked the Aerosmith/Run DMC collaboration too. It was compelling because you could see the common elements of two genres that seemed quite different, but it was that much more apparent that they really come from more or less the same place," I said. "Kinda like me and you, actually."

Garvey smiled. "Who's Chuck D and who's Flavor Flav?"

"Dude, come on," I responded. "I'm definitely Flav."

CHAPTER 13

La La

"You ready?" Garvey asked with a glint in his eye. This could only mean one thing.

"Yes, I am," I replied.

"It could take about an hour before they kick in, so let's eat them now."

Garvey produced the little beige earplugs and put one in my hand, and looked right into my eyes. It was a bit like looking at Richard Ramirez at that moment. But I'd seen this look before.

There was that time in Toronto when we decided to hit a Taco Bell in the middle of the night. We brought our acoustic guitars, because we thought it would be funny to play that little Spanish flamenco rumba strumming thing you hear in commercials for the fine people at Taco Bell. There was no question in my mind afterwards that the kids in the back preparing our burritos spit in them quite generously in response to this drunken musical presentation. We'd have been lucky if they limited their donations to simply saliva. But Garvey insisted on this, with that same look, and I was right there with him. I wasn't about to say no this time either.

"Down the hatch, Jensen," Garvey hooted as he popped his portion into his mouth and washed it down with a beer. There was a very brief moment that could been considered a Mexican standoff as he watched me ingest mine. It was like a schoolyard pact. After I swallowed, there was no turning back.

Garvey returned to his chair, which at that moment was perfectly positioned under the skylight so as to immerse both he and the chair in a perfectly vertical tractor beam of sunlight. Better to see this now than after the mushrooms took hold.

"Alright, whose turn is it?" I asked.

"I believe it is your turn, friend," Garvey said.

I got up and grabbed my iPod, scrolling down the playlist to find out what my next selection would be. Ah yes. *This* song.

It was probably my most honest addition, my biggest leap. I would have been lying to myself had I not included it here. I had to.

Ka-chik.

Garvey's face immediately soured at the overproduction he heard.

"What the hell is this?"

"It's KISS. The song is called "Sure Know Something"."

"What album?"

"*Dynasty*. 1979."

One of his eyebrows rose to break up the sourness a bit.

"I have to be honest with myself," I started. "I can't deny my compulsion for this song."

"Go on."

"Okay, listen. KISS music is dumb. Everyone knows that. Even KISS has admitted that. But this song from Paul Stanley, man. All the planets lined up, all the variables, the timing...everything. It hit me square in the chest as a twelve year old KISS fanatic."

"You should write him a letter," Garvey mockingly encouraged.

"You're funny," I answered.

"This song succeeds almost in spite of itself, inside the scrambling mess that the KISS enterprise was at that time," I continued. "If we're really being honest, most KISS songs written after 1978 are bullshit, particularly ones written around this time. Superficially, "Sure Know Something" is a finely crafted pop song with a catchy hook, and the consideration would typically just stop there. Yeah, it's slick and way overproduced, and sure, you can say that artistic sophistication may be lacking."

"I will say that," Garvey responded.

"But here's the important thing. Even in complete acceptance of these facts, not to mention that as a KISS fan since childhood I have sooooo many other songs I could choose from in their catalogue, others seemingly much more important, I still can't deny that this song significantly stirs my emotions. I try hard to make a point of separating intellectual criticism from any emotional connection I might have with music that I love, and this song is a great example of why it's important to do that."

Garvey leaned forward. "Right."

"One of the most wonderful things music can do for you is to act as a conduit that closes the gap between the person you are and the person you wish you were, or want to be. And not many bands did that better than KISS. I wanted to be that guy in the song. As weird as it sounds, I wanted to be a guy who could identify with those experiences with girls, and feel those feelings. I wanted involvement. I wanted to believe. I was about to transition into a teenager and I was just starting to really notice girls, and this song just got to me at precisely the right time. I had already been under KISS' power for a few years, and their warm familiarity prompted me to be even more receptive to this song as a kid just coming into his teens."

Garvey nodded affirmatively.

"In the promotional video, all of the standard and beloved KISS totems came together to compel me. And the most important of all was Ace Frehley's trademark puckered-lips swagger while he played the chugging power chords coming into the chorus of this song - defiant and without fear."

I paused for a moment, in thought.

"And you know what, Garvey? That's what this whole thing was all about, right there," I said.

"What?"

"I wanted to be fearless too."

Garvey and I looked at each other for what felt like more than just one moment, and he nodded silently. He understood what I was trying to say.

"Let's change gears a little with a song written about your wife," Garvey offered.

"What?"

Elvis Costello's "Alison" was his next song.

"Ah. Okay. I'm relieved to hear that it wasn't "Baby Got Back"," I said. "Alison would be very happy to know that you included this song in your playlist," I said.

"And equally disappointed to learn that you did not," he responded.

"You don't know that for sure, smartass."

Garvey and I still had a lot of songs to show off to each other. I figured we were likely forty to fifty songs in at this point. I didn't really remember the back end of my playlist, but it seemed to me that it was about to become increasingly varied if memory served.

"I love Costello's voice, and I love his songs. They're simple enough to be accessible and yet complicated enough that you probably couldn't play them properly," Garvey said of his selection.

"I love his old stuff, like *Armed Forces*. And actually, that record he did with The Roots recently gets a lot of airtime at my place too. You ever watch that show Costello hosted a few years back, where he would have musical guests on and informally interview them?" I asked.

"Yeah, the one with Springsteen was my favourite. They're sitting around talking like two old buddies on barstools over a beer. Springsteen tells Costello that he was always watching to see what Costello would release next, and that he felt like he had to constantly play catch-up with him, like they were competing. Springsteen said he would always try to make his next record that much better than what Costello had just put out," Garvey replied.

"Yeah, I saw that one too. High praise. I wish that show was still on," I said to Garvey on his way to the bathroom.

Time for my next song.

Ka-chik.

"Nice pick!" Garvey shouted from the latrine.

It was Led Zeppelin's "Good Times Bad Times". I smiled to myself.

"The sheer power this band had, especially at the outset, likely just flat out scared a lot of people," I said.

"I read a great story recently about Jimmy Page remixing this song," Garvey said as he sat back down in his chair. "He said he was listening intently to the song for the first time in many years, and he said to himself, '*hey - this band was pretty fucking good, man*'. I thought that was great."

"That's funny. Jeez, do you think, Jimmy?" I responded. "It must have been incredible to be around to experience Led Zeppelin unfold the way they did back then, to literally watch the musical landscape change right before your eyes."

"Exciting times, without doubt."

Garvey's next song was also a classic. The Beatles' "Hey Jude".

"Listen to this. McCartney melodies are unbeatable," he enthused. "And the chorus and vocal outro are positively irresistible. Paul busts out his rock voice for the greatest ad-lib vocal riffing in rock history - *Jooo-Jooody-Jooody-Jooody-Jooody-Jooody-YOW!*"

I smiled and nodded in acknowledgement of Garvey's excitement as this track played out. He was really loving this, and I was glad.

"And this is a *na-na* song. You know how I feel about a good *na-na* song versus a *la-la* song," he mused.

"Hey, my position stands," I responded. "McCartney could get away with doing *la-la*, but he knows the difference too."

This exchange had to do with a topic we had discussed previously about a theory I had. My theory was that singing *la-la* evoked more femininity than singing *na-na* did. Go ahead - sing a couple to yourself and you'll see what I mean. Singing *la, la, la* just feels more feminine. Not that there's anything wrong with that, of course.

"You know how in the French language, every noun has a gender?" I asked Garvey.

"Uh, not really. But go on."

"They do, and it dictates whether the pronoun used is *le*, for masculine words, or *la*, for feminine words."

"*Liar!*" Garvey heckled in that voice.

"No, seriously. I'm not kidding. There's no distinct connection, but the notion that *la* sounds feminine is valid. Say *oooh la la*."

Garvey twisted up his face at me. "No! What's wrong with you?"

"I'm trying to prove a point. It sounds super fem."

"What about *oooh na na*?"

"Nobody would ever say that," I reasoned.

"*La* and *na* are the exact same thing."

"They do seem the same, but they're not. I do agree that the difference is subtle," I said, pausing and then continuing with an attempt to further clarify my point.

"Look at it this way. The difference between *la la la* and *na na na* is actually kinda like the head nod greeting versus the lifted chin greeting," I continued.

"What are you talking about?" Garvey was becoming impatient.

"Say you're walking down the street, and a stranger passes you. If he nods his head downward, it implies a quiet respect. If he flicks his head back and directs his chin up towards you instead, it implies a more aggressive engagement, like *'hey, what's up with you'*. It's more open ended, whereas the downward head nod is dismissive - *'hello, I must be on my way. No need for us to talk.'* They *seem* like the same thing, but they're totally different," I theorized.

"Can I give you the downward head nod right now to end this conversation?"

"Only if you admit that *la* is more fem that *na*."

"Put your next goddamn song on," Garvey smirked.

"Did you know that women sometimes refer to their lady parts as their *la la*?"

"Okay, really. That's enough now."

My next selection was an artist double-play. More Zeppelin. This was "Friends", from their third record.

"Nice track," Garvey said.

"I like that Zeppelin could make an acoustic album like *Led Zeppelin III* and not face any derision. They made this record on their own terms. I love the intended simplicity of it, even though from a technical standpoint Page's playing was hard to follow with all of his bizarre tunings," I said.

This song seemed to meld perfectly with the sunlight shining down on us through the windows. When it ended, Garvey got up and replaced my iPod with his. He had a peculiar look on his face as he looked at me and pressed play.

"Brace yourself, pilgrim," Garvey warned.

My jaw dropped in reaction to the perversion I was hearing.

"You're kidding, right?" I asked.

I always knew that my friend Garvey's musical tastes were vast. It was a fact that had been reinforced by this exercise. He loved soul, and he loved the blues. I learned that he even listened to Ratt and Judas Priest at one point in his life. But for him to include George Michael's "Father Figure" in his playlist left me stymied.

"Wow. Please explain this," I said.

"I know you hate it. But I can't help but love it. It's soulful."

"I feel like George Michael is a soulless charlatan," I replied.

"So you're saying you don't like his music then?"

The smile that appeared on my face felt wicked.

"I'm saying that the only thing I could have ever liked about George Michael was that he put himself in a position where he was able to bang Linda Evangelista, and he wasn't even able to do that."

That comment may have been a bit too aggressive.

"Well, this is a guilty pleasure. We all have them. You have them. We just played one of yours," Garvey said.

He was right. Here I had just gone on about "Sure Know Something", and now I was giving him a hard time.

"Pop music can be like a musical handjob," Garvey acquiesced, and we both laughed together. "What's next on your fucking playlist, you hypocrite?"

"Funny you should ask," I responded. "No shit, this is really what's next!"

I brought the iPod over to show him in case he didn't believe me. My next song was "Pop Muzik" by M. Garvey shrugged his shoulders. I walked back to the dock, inserted my iPod and pushed play.

Clearly the mushrooms were controlling our devices.

"Oh, okay. I know this. What, or who, is 'M'?" Garvey asked.

"It's the name of a project by a guy named Robin Scott."

"Musical handjobs…." Garvey noted.

"Indeed. U2 actually opened their shows on the *PopMart* tour with this song," I added.

"Makes perfect sense, doesn't it?"

I smiled. "Yep. Your turn."

"We're going to continue down our unusual path with this tune," Garvey offered.

His next song was a country-tinged version of "The Scientist". It started with a pedal steel guitar and an acoustic that sounded like its strings needed to be changed. What I heard next perplexed me. Garvey was full of surprises all of a sudden.

"No fucking way," I blurted. "Is that…*Willie Nelson?*"

"Yes, it is. I'd heard the Coldplay version a hundred times and it didn't turn me on at all. I heard Willie's version once and I fell in love. It's not just that I prefer his voice over Chris Martin's. It's the interpretation, the weariness Willie breathes into the song," Garvey said.

I like Chris Martin, but Garvey was right. Initially Nelson's voice in this song was like an aberration to my ears for the first few lines of the vocal. It didn't seem right. But then, I could hear an interesting new fragility. I could hear all of Nelson's years in his voice, every heartbreak, every failure. Every compromise.

The creaking honesty of Willie Nelson's warble sought to represent the wide chasm between the musical impressions Garvey and I have always had. I had been conditioned to recognize musical value in competency, technical excellence, and in overtly obvious skill supremacy. He saw perfection in earnestness and integrity.

For me, weakness simply meant inferiority. But in Garvey's music, weakness could demonstrate a certain strength. A nobility.

I had infused my own emotion into songs to try to make them my own, and Garvey did the reverse. He borrowed emotion from his. He never wanted to own the songs. He wanted them to own him.

CHAPTER 14

Long Live Punk

"I'm feeling something additional to what I should be feeling from just the booze," Garvey said.

He was waiting for the mushrooms to come on. I was halfway through the label of my current wine bottle, a satisfied recipient of a nice, easy late-afternoon buzz. Switching over to what was left in that bottle of scotch on the kitchen counter after dinner would sharpen me up for my sojourn into this night.

Maybe best to get food out of the way now.

"We should probably eat something soon. Wanna try the barbecue?" I asked.

"Sure."

We walked the distance from our cabin to the grill on elastic legs.

"Looks like we have some neighbours," Garvey said quietly, gesturing with his eyes. I looked to the right of our cabin, and saw a couple sitting on the front porch of their own cabin in the distance.

"Shall we bring over a pie?" I offered.

"We need to be on our best behaviour," Garvey deliberated.

I looked at him. A sly smirk crossed his lips, his eyes indicating that he was now fully switched on.

"Blast off, Colonel Garvin," I said.

"To infinity, *and beyond!*" Garvey yelped.

So much for the best behaviour.

We confirmed that the barbecue was in working condition this time, turning it up to full and returning to the cabin for the meat.

And then it all came back to me.

That ease of laughter as a result of most anything you witness.

Anything.

Barbecue tongs being manipulated by human hands take on peculiar quirks and hilarious new meanings.

Logic briefly attempted to assert itself, but failed. There was a vague struggle with the notion that these things should not have been the least bit funny, and yet were.

Our immediate situation reminded me of an old Batman comic I read as a kid. It was the issue that had The Joker releasing some form of elixir into the drinking water supply of Gotham City that converted everyone's mouths into ghoulish and painful-looking bright red-lipped smiles. As the victims laughed themselves to death, they writhed and struggled to control themselves, but were unable to do so. The artwork was bizarre and sinister, and it coupled with the contextual irony to etch itself into my impressionable young mind.

I knew there wasn't anything particularly funny about what we were doing, but now I couldn't control myself either. As we stood at the barbecue preparing our food, any eye contact whatsoever between Garvey and me would initiate a substantial laughing fit. There was a lot of eye contact, but not many words exchanged. We didn't have to talk. Primitive facial expressions conveyed anything that was essential.

Trying to eat a meal on mushrooms is a fool's prospect. Dangerous, even. I don't remember much of what was said over the course of our dinner. I just remember the incessant laughing. I do remember that at one point I was bent over in my chair with a mouthful of food and my face close to the floor, unable to breathe, begging for mercy from the hilarity lest I would choke to death.

The Joker had spiked our mushrooms. For a two and a half second span there was complete blackness and it felt like my life shut itself off for that period of time.

Soon after, I was able to pull it together enough to tell a story.

"Do you know who Gavin DeGraw is?" I asked Garvey after regaining my composure.

"Yep. This is him, right? "Chariot"?"

"Yeah."

I had let my iPod play through a separate playlist during dinner.

"He does the song "I Don't Want To Be" too. Great songs, incredible singer," I said.

"So Alison and I were visiting a friend and his family one weekend in Connecticut at their summer home," I continued. "My friend is in the entertainment business and he has a number of celebrity pals. Early on the Saturday night, he looks up from his Blackberry and says, '*Ah, looks like Gavin is coming over later tonight*'. I thought nothing of it, because that was all he said. I imagined this person was just a neighbour dropping by for a few drinks. So we're outside at the back of the property, and from around the corner comes this thin, unshaven guy with a Converse ball cap, dark t-shirt, and a pair of black jeans and sneakers. My buddy Ian greets him, and then he introduces his friend Gavin to the rest of us. Gavin is soft-spoken and shy, and mostly sticks around Ian."

"What did you do?" Garvey intoned with a parent's disapproval, and another laughing fit comes on. After a few minutes, I continued the story.

"So Ian's father-in-law takes us out to dinner at a nice restaurant in downtown Mystic…"

"Mystic as in *Mystic Pizza*?" Garvey cut in.

"Yes, actually. The pizza place is still there. We took a picture of it."

"You're totally lying about all of this!" Garvey choked, beside himself with laughter.

"Pull it together, man! Come on. I'm trying to get through this story."

I could barely stop laughing myself.

"Okay, okay. Keep going," Garvey sputtered, looking at me with a suspicious smile.

"Where was I now? I forget." I started laughing.

Christ.

"You were telling that lie about *Mystic Pizza*."

I tilted my head sideways. "Come on."

"Alright, go. Continue."

"Okay, so…there's a party of about seven or eight of us at this very nice bistro-type restaurant. We finish dinner and Gavin excuses himself from the table, presumably to use the washroom. When he gets back to the table, Ian's father-in-law Jason says to him, '*nice try, my friend*'. Gavin had tried to pick up the tab for everyone's meals before Jason could take care of it. I wondered to myself, *what must this guy do for a living?* He just looked like some young dude off the street."

"Yesssss..." Garvey hissed like Montgomery Burns, trying to make me laugh.

"We get back to the house and continue with the drinks, and I see that Gavin had brought an acoustic guitar with him. Alison and I still have *no idea* who he is. An hour or so later, I ask Gavin to break out the guitar so that we could jam. He politely declines, saying he's just learning how to play. But I'm pretty buzzed and I say, *'that's okay, I'll play and you can sing. Come on man, it'll be fun!'* Everyone is right there, but I don't pick up on anything weird."

Garvey winced. "Ugh."

"Yeah. So he very politely declines. He's very meek. I just thought he wasn't confident enough to play in front of people or something. Hah! As the night wore on and the drinks flowed, this stuff continued. I didn't see him the next day, as he had left before we got up."

"You're a schmuck," Garvey said.

"I know, but listen. The week after Alison and I got home, I saw a clip of him presenting at the American Music Awards. I yelled to Alison, *'Holy crap, there's that guy! It's fucking Gavin!'* And they played "I Don't Want To Be", a song that had already been on my iPod because I liked it. I knew "Chariot" too. But I had no idea that it was *him*, the entire time! *Can you fucking believe that?!?!?!"* I shouted at Garvey, who was bent over and holding his abdomen, howling with laughter.

"I felt so horrible about the whole thing, especially the guitar bit. I was so embarrassed. I texted Ian and begged him to explain and apologize to Gavin on my behalf," I wheezed.

"Jackass," Garvey said after we caught our breath.

My next song was perfect for our current mood. It was my favourite 80s pop song, "Our House" by the UK group Madness.

"Wow," Garvey said. *"Really?"*

"Really," I responded. "This song immediately improves my mood no matter what. The pep of the horns, the tongue-in-cheek delivery, and that English ska vibe. I love it all. I liked a lot of this stuff early on - The English Beat, The Specials, Madness, and later, bands like Fishbone. This stuff was happy music on the surface, but it had grit at the same time. This was actually one of the first videos I had ever seen, and I've always cherished the memory of it. It's an upbeat video for an upbeat, clever song."

The Madness song balanced out some of the melancholy of my playlist. It's possible that there was a subconscious takeaway on my part from this video as a kid. It was shot mostly in the living room of an old Victorian terraced house, the working-class kind that were all sombrely linked together under dismal English overcast skies. The video conveyed a sentiment that happiness was possible regardless of your environment.

I recognized that distinct flavour of happiness back then in songs like "Our House" and "Wake Me Up (Before You Go-Go)", but I turned my back on it in favour of darker, more aggressive and seemingly more powerful songs, because that was the music that the identity I wanted back then called for. Darkness was always more compelling than light. I just couldn't find myself in a Wham! song. It was more interesting to look for the answers in a Metallica dirge instead. That's where I felt I identified most; where I thought I was most comfortable as a teen. I tried on various personalities as a kid, and I eventually wore the one that fit best. It was all about looking for those elusive answers then, even if I wasn't really even consciously aware that I was.

Christ, who was I kidding? It's still about looking for the answers. Probably always will be.

After all, that's really what I was doing here.

Garvey's next selection was by REM, a band that hid their taciturn darkness inside pop song snark. I liked them, and I should have liked them much earlier in my life.

"I love REM, but I find it hard to land on a single song that sums up my love for them. This one comes closest," he said. The song he described was "Driver 8".

"It's the clean, reverby guitar lick that gets me I think," he added.

"I'm pretty sure I have an REM song coming up at some point too," I said. "They were like a punk band without the outward punk obviousness."

"You just summed up college radio," Garvey laughed.

I got up and replaced his iPod with mine in the dock. "You'd never hear *this* on college radio."

Speak of the devils, and they shall appear in your playlist.

Metallica.

I had always felt a physiological response to great metal songs. The best ones always set the tone by beginning with an anticipatory buildup, and this next one had one of the better examples of that dramatic buildup in all of heavy metal. The problem was that this wasn't technically a heavy metal song *per se*. In actual fact, it was Metallica covering a song by post-punk outfit Killing Joke. For me, this was only part of an ironic juxtaposition surrounding this song.

"This song presents me with an interesting conundrum, frère," I told Garvey as the monstrous riff leapt out of the sound dock, lumbering through our chalet like a musical Godzilla threatening to destroy all that lie in its path.

"What's the conundrum?" Garvey asked.

"This is a song from a record of cover tunes Metallica put out almost as a gag. It was recorded by the band in Lars Ulrich's garage in El Cerrito," I started.

"Yeah, I'm familiar with it."

"You are?"

"Yeah, but go on," Garvey offered.

"Technically, it's not a real Metallica album. But sometimes I wonder if it's my favourite Metallica album based on how much I absolutely love most of the songs on it. I could never bring myself to admit that, because it seems a bit perverse."

"Sounds like you might have some issues to work out," Garvey mocked.

"I think I might. But I've been clinging to the notion that the reason I like the album so much is because it incorporates all of the things I love about Metallica. That it's really *Metallica* that makes this record special, beyond the fact that Metallica wasn't responsible for writing any of the songs."

"And you like these songs better than any other song from their other *real* records?" he questioned.

"I would never admit that."

"Seems blasphemous to me."

He was preying on my concerns now, that fucker. Winding me up.

"Screw off. We'll just leave it at that," I smiled. "But you said you were familiar with this record. How's that?"

"I used to hang out with this guy."

"What guy? From Sudbury? Did I know him?"

"Well, I don't know if I actually *hung out* with him as much as I would just find myself in his company the way you often did in your adventures as a teenager. But man, he used to love this album. He had a car back then, and he would rip up the dark gravel roads of the outskirts of Sudbury at night with his lights off, doing a hundred and fifty with this album cranked as loud as it would go. I was on hand for one or two of those rides. I was scared to death, yelling at him to turn the goddamn lights back on, and he would just laugh like a lunatic," Garvey shared.

"Metallica tends to bring out the lunatic in all of us," I said. "You're up."

Garvey pressed play on his next tune. Definitely a change of gears. Elton John's "Goodbye Yellow Brick Road".

"I could have a dozen Elton John songs in this collection, but this was my favourite at the time of creating this playlist. This could be because I don't own this record and I only hear this song when it's in a movie, and seemingly it's in one of every four movies I see. But man, on soundtracks this song works in damn near any situation," Garvey explained.

I thought about that for a minute as I listened.

"It really does, doesn't it? Elton John songs seem to have that timelessness about them. "Tiny Dancer", "Rocket Man"…" I added.

"Yep."

"I only really know the hits too. But Elton would probably have a lot of great deep tracks to dig into from his old records, particularly the ones from the early 70s."

"Did Bernie Taupin write the lyrics first, or did Elton write the music first?" Garvey asked.

"Not sure. I think I read somewhere that both the lyrics and the music were done separately at the same time, and then they were combined and crafted into songs."

"Makes sense," Garvey said.

"I do know that Elton played piano on two tracks for Saxon's *Rock the Nations* record in the 80s."

"You would know that," Garvey exhaled.

•

This musical discourse between Garvey and I wasn't anything I could really experience anywhere else. I could do this for ages. One day Garvey and I would likely share a room in a retirement facility with all of our music, kibitzing back and forth about the cultural ramifications of Slayer's Kerry King playing guitar on The Beastie Boys' "No Sleep 'Til Brooklyn". And we'd likely still be addressing each other as 'motherfucker'.

My next song would definitely elicit a positive response from ol' Garvin. It was "Don't Let It Bring You Down", the first of two consecutive Neil Young songs in my playlist.

"Beautiful!" he yelled from the bathroom.

"I love that second chord he goes to in the verses of this song," I said to him when he returned to his chair.

"What is that, like an A?"

"I don't remember. It's some derivative of an A chord I think. It's perfect, it catches your attention and adds that little nuance that Neil does so well."

"He certainly uses some bizarre chords," Garvey said.

"Yeah. What's cool is that it's almost as though he uses the available chord language but then makes tweaks based on the melodies he's looking for. He does that a lot," I said. "Kinda like Dave Matthews, but Matthews took all that to a whole other place. I think Matthews just made up his own chords."

"Yeah, he did. His songs are ridiculous to try and learn," Garvey agreed.

"I remember when you came by my house with that Dave Matthews and Tim Reynolds live record in the late 90s, and we just sat and listened to the guitars in awe over and over again."

"Right. And then we played some Stones on guitar," Garvey laughed as he got up to change out the iPods.

"This is Otis Redding, and the song is called "These Arms of Mine"," Garvey said. "There are few voices I like better than Otis'. If I could sing like anyone, it might be him. I actually fell in love with a version of this done by Willie and the Poor Boys, which was a brief 'supergroup' that included Paul Rodgers and Jimmy Page at one point back in the mid-80s."

"You mean The Firm?" I asked.

"No, I don't think so."

I didn't know enough about The Firm to interject further.

"Anyway, I followed the roots back and that was my introduction to Otis Redding. His version of "Satisfaction" almost made my list. Keith Richards says that Otis' version is how he intended "Satisfaction" to sound - the same riff, but played with horns."

I nodded my head in approval. "It's nice. Great rasp at the end."

My second Neil Young track, "Sugar Mountain", was next.

Ka-chik.

"This song reminds me of all of the special times I've had sitting around with the acoustic," I told Garvey. "The lyrics for this song run directly parallel to my experience living in dorm at university. I always imagined the song as being about my time there - how much I learned, how glorious it was, how quickly it passed and then how incredibly heartbreaking it was to have to leave. That lyric that goes, '*you can't be twenty, on Sugar Mountain*'; we were getting too old to be at school any longer. We had to graduate and move on, and on our way out, we watched the young kids coming in to take our places. What a painful consideration that is, isn't it? One night towards the end, just before we graduated, a bunch of us were sitting around and I was playing "Sugar Mountain" on guitar and singing the words, and we all felt that same brand of sadness together. One of the guys got up and walked away with tears in his eyes."

"I'm afraid your playing has had that same effect on me too, Jensen," Garvey said.

I shook my head.

"It's your turn, you heartless cretin," I replied.

I didn't know the specific name of the song that Garvey had just started, but I did know the band. I remembered that the video had alarmed me back in high school.

"Never mind my playing. This guy's teeth made *me* cry," I said to Garvey. "This is The Pogues, yes?"

"Yes, it is. "Fairytale of New York"," he answered.

"Alright, proceed."

"Shane McGowan is like Bob Dylan in Ireland, an idea I can only understand when I listen to this song. I noticed something when compiling this list - I like songs that embrace juxtaposition in some way. Like when the Velvets sing pretty songs about heroin overdoses. This song's like that. It's a booze-fuelled argument between conflicted lovers on Christmas Day, all set to a traditional folk song," Garvey explained.

"Not my thing, but I hear what you're saying," I offered.

The sun had gone down some time ago, and the cold darkness outside our windows urged a fire. Other than the couple in the cabin across the way, there was no one else out here in the blackness. Just the friends we chose to invite in through our iPods. Our next friend brought a glimmer of daytime sunshine in with him.

"Is this Nik Kershaw?" Garvey asked after I hit play.

"Yes it is, sir."

"This is a great song. I'm surprised you like this."

"Because it's a great song?"

"Because it's not Van Halen."

"Bah! I've always liked this song. It brings back very vivid memories from high school," I said.

Like "Our House", this song always brightened me up. Always had.

"I think our playlists are dating each other again," Garvey suggested. His next song was Roxy Music's "More Than This".

"Someday I'll take the time to dive into Brian Eno's catalogue. Until then I only know the hits. This song, like the other Roxy Music songs I know, is pretty and haunting without being sad," Garvey reflected.

Haunting, *without being sad.*

I stared at the floor for a moment. I had taken in everything that Garvey had said about his music during our time here, but this comment particularly piqued my attention. I knew what he meant by it, but I still felt as though there was more to know. What was his perception of *sad*? Was it the same as mine?

People typically have varying ideas about what being *happy* means, while we all find it easier to identify with a common sense of what being *sad* is. But here within the confines of our musical association, there was likely some variance to be mulled over. I wanted some additional granularity on this topic, some detail.

At that moment though, I decided to just let it pass. Maybe it would come up again later. If it didn't, I would bring it up. I needed to explore the aspects of my jones for the inclusion of sadness in music within the paradigm of what we were doing out here.

"Your turn," Garvey said from his chair.

Interesting. My next song may have been similar to his last selection in that it was also haunting, and yet not overtly sad. Actually, it seemed hopeful in spite of an observation that may be construed as sad, if you really wanted to see it as such. But surprisingly, I never had. The song was called "All My Favorite People", by a group called Over The Rhine.

"I love this," Garvey commented during the first chorus.

"It has a very calming warmth about it," I replied.

It reminded me of that saxophone-led musical piece the band always played at the end of *Saturday Night Live* when everyone gathered on the main stage around the guest host to take their final bows. I'd always wished I had a full album of just *that*.

"Who is this?"

"They're called Over The Rhine. Very little known as far as I can tell. And I hope they stay that way."

"Why?"

"Because popularity will negatively impact their creativity. History tells us this time and time again, Garvey," I said. "Purity is lost. When bands get popular, purity gets lost and I feel like they don't belong to me any longer. And I don't want them anymore."

"That's the punk ethos, my friend."

"Yeah? Then long live punk, motherfucker."

CHAPTER 15

The Song Remains The Same

Garvey's next song was "The Wind Cries Mary", by Jimi Hendrix. Before we came out here, I had talked to someone about the general idea for this exercise, explaining it in broad strokes but with the required amount of specificity to make my point. This initiated an obvious general question, in turn followed by a couple of more pointedly specific ones.

The general question was of a qualifying quality - *'what are some of the songs in your playlist?'*

After I answered that question, a more specific question was directed - *'do you have any Jimi Hendrix in your playlist?'*

When my answer was issued in the negative, the next question was, *'how could you not have any Jimi Hendrix in your playlist?'*

The question irked me slightly, tempting me to answer with a question of my own. It would have been, *'why don't you come up with your own fucking playlist?'*

Of course, the Hendrix question was only volleyed as a lighthearted gibe, likely intended to promote extended conversation. But my concern with this had always been in the initial purpose, which I was very careful to clarify.

My playlist had to consist of music that stirs a special emotive feeling in me, and I was probably sensitive because I strove to maintain that a certain purity had to be emphasized. I could really like a song, or maybe even love it, as I did songs by Faster Pussycat or Chuck Prophet. But it was possible that these songs just didn't ignite that special, marked physiological response that took me to another level. And for me, if they didn't they couldn't be included.

The whole point was to move away from artist exaltation lists based on pre-established conceptions, or popularity contests. The intention was not to celebrate Led Zeppelin's "Stairway to Heaven" out of some obligatory showing of rock royalty respect. If a song didn't elicit that special response, then it just...*didn't*. I was admittedly self-conscious about this premise. Maybe because it was so personal.

I like Jimi Hendrix and his music, and I certainly appreciate his massive musical contributions. But he never really lit me up in any special way, the way he did Garvey. And this point leads to a secondary, deeper application of this enterprise - did I feel the need to justify feelings for my own music against Garvey's (or anyone else's) to realize some form of normalcy or equality? Did I need to quell an inadequacy I may have felt for my emotions where this music was concerned? This was the entire point here, why I was doing all of this - to try to gain a greater understanding of the feelings themselves and where they come from, and to come to peace with that understanding. Garvey's own opinion and potential divergence served as a litmus test not just against my preferences, but against my own personal feelings.

As "The Wind Cried Mary" played, Garvey provided his take on the song.

"People think of Jimi Hendrix and they think screaming guitars and feedback. In fact, a considerable portion of Hendrix's playing is clean bell-like tones, and this song captures that. These compositions are on par with Mozart for me. And Jimi wasn't a terribly good singer but his voice is 'real', so you don't really notice."

After the song had ended, I'll admit that I did like it more than I had previously. But there was no special emotive response. And I knew there wouldn't be. My feeling remained the same; I was untouched. But I was that much closer to understanding why.

CHAPTER 16

All My Favourite People Are Broken

My next song was one that I could listen to over and over again, Ozark Mountain Daredevils' "Jackie Blue". It's a 70s gem that was initially written about drugs, but at the insistence of the record company, it was re-engineered to be about a 'girl'. The song is sung not by the band's singer, but instead by their drummer Larry Lee. He sings the song in a higher register, making it almost sound like it's being sung by a woman.

These are the only things I know about this band, as the remainder of their song catalogue sounds nothing like "Jackie Blue" thus warranting no further interest on my part.

"Is this a dude singing?" Garvey asked.

"Yep. He sings so high that it's deceiving, right? Same way that Wayne Newton did on "Danke Schoen". I had a bet with someone once that "Danke Schoen" wasn't performed by a woman. And the bet was *with* a woman," I said.

"What was the bet for?" Garvey asked.

"A woman."

"By a woman, with a woman, for a woman. Makes sense."

A woman was not what the bet was for, obviously. It was for twenty bucks. And it took place long before the advent of the interwebs.

We listened to the song's conclusion, and Garvey got up to switch in. "Was the woman's name Jackie Blue?"

"Which woman?"

"Okay, enough of your nonsense. Listen up," Garvey chided as he pressed play. A Simon & Garfunkel song emerged.

"This is "The Boxer"," he announced before I could hazard a guess. "What a beautiful story. Better lyrics are hard to find. More juxtaposition here - pretty melodies and harmonies combined with sad and lonely characters."

"I prefer Paul Simon's later solo stuff to his material with Art Garfunkel," I said, trying to sound as non-oppositional as possible. I was still very much interested in the contents of Garvey's playlist, as much as I was in his perceptions of said playlist.

I loved that every new song to come held deep possibilities. This aspect of the exercise was compelling enough in itself. When a new song was in line with the previous one in terms of genre or style, it was interesting. When it ran completely counter, that was also interesting. Even when I looked down at my iPod and it produced a song that I knew that Garvey would hate, *that* was interesting.

I pressed play on The Police's "Canary in a Coal Mine" next. I had loved this song from the very first time I heard it in my second year of university.

"This is a very unique selection," Garvey said. "I'm learning a lot about you and your deviant mind."

"One of the benefits of this excursion, frère."

"Canary in a Coal Mine" seemed to be over before it started. I ran over to the sound dock to remove my iPod before my next song was exposed. We had been a little lax in punching in and punching out at this point. A post-mushroom lethargy had presented itself. Garvey got up and punched in as I visited the bathroom. From in there, I heard a voice that squinted my eyes.

"Who the fuck is that singing?" I yelled out to Garvey.

"Tom Waits. This is "Downtown Train"," he yelled back.

"What's with his bloody voice?"

Garvey chose not to answer my question directly.

"This is in the group of my favourite songs ever. There ain't much orchestration - barely audible bass and sparse snare drum, some fantastic piercing guitar licks, and Waits' inimitable growl. That prick Rod Stewart nearly ruined this song for me after wiping his ass with it."

I laughed at Garvey's abrupt animosity.

"Jeez, man. Pretty aggressive. What did Rod Stewart ever do to you?"

"It's what he did to perfectly good songs. All that *American Songbook* stuff was complete bullshit."

"Yeah, I can see that."

Rod Stewart's "Baby Jane" had spent a brief period of time on my list of guilty non-metal song pleasures back in the 80s. I thought it was catchy.

"I'm sorry man, but Tom Waits' voice is not cool..." I started.

"*Judgment*...," Garvey urged.

"...for me," I finished. "It's very, very unusual."

My playlist seemed to be jumping all over the place now, more than it had previously. Canadian band Prism's "Armageddon" was up next. The overblown intro to the song began, an intro that could have only been possible in the late 70s. And maybe in the 80s too, I guess.

"Who's this?" Garvey questioned.

"Keep listening. I don't want to tell you, I think you'll know it. I also don't want to tell you in advance for fear of any bias."

Garvey frowned and took a gulp of whatever was in his glass.

The vocal line came in, but still nothing. Garvey had no idea. And usually the vocal is the last line of detection.

"Alright, I don't know who this is. Tell me."

"It's Prism. "Armageddon"."

Garvey nodded uneventfully.

"My first exposure to Prism was when I was ten, and in a sense this was like an introduction to rock for me. I felt like this was the beginning of the rock that was to come. It seemed big and more powerful to me back then. It was slick and overproduced, but that just made it more palatable for a kid my age," I said.

"What about KISS? Wasn't that your introduction?"

"KISS music wasn't quite so real to me when I was ten, in that it was only a small part of what KISS actually represented in the 70s - more of a visual spectacle. It was like this continually unfolding panoramic. I paid more attention to their costume development and their characters than I did to their music when I was younger. The music was more or less just the soundtrack to the spectacle. Almost like that little bit of music that played during those Silver Shamrock commercials in *Halloween III - Season of the Witch*."

Garvey laughed. "*Happy happy Halloween, Silver Shamrock,*" he sang.

"Right. The context was the same for me. The music was almost just an ad, like bait to get your attention and draw you in to the real purpose," I reasoned.

"And that was?" Garvey knew the answer.

"Handing over your money for the mountains of merchandising. The invitation to be brainwashed was there with both KISS and Silver Shamrock, but the only difference was that the Ace Frehley Halloween mask didn't turn my head into a smouldering pile of insects and snakes."

"That's what KISS' music was for," Garvey responded as he grabbed a bottle of wine from the counter and lifted it in my direction. "You a white guy?"

"When I'm at the clubs I sometimes feel as though I'm a black guy. But yes homie, I am a white guy."

No approval from Garvey.

"Want some or not, funny man?"

"No thanks."

I was in fact a red guy, and had just opened a fresh bottle of it that was somewhere in the chalet. I would locate it eventually.

Garvey pressed play on his next song and headed back into the kitchen.

"Oh my. *Again!?!*" I said in disbelief.

"Yes, again. This song makes me want to take off my shirt and wave my hands in the air during the gospel-like chorus."

George Michael had made his return in Garvey's playlist, this time in the form of his single "Freedom".

As the chorus rang out, Garvey jumped in the air dramatically in full jazz hands flourish in front of the window. From my chair I looked over his shoulder, and I could see the couple in the next chalet observing his dance routine from their front porch.

"If there was any doubt before, it's gone now," I laughed and nodded toward the window to advise Garvey of his audience. He turned around to face them, and then shouted out the song's flamboyant refrain at full volume, repeating his jazz hands move with even more flair. I was laughing so hard I could barely breathe. "Freedom" was like a plastic flower to me. It meant less than nothing. This was the most enjoyment I would derive from it.

"Your turn, bitch. Can you top that?" Garvey said to me.

"Before I even look at my playlist, I'm going to say I really doubt it," I replied.

My next song was a more sensible pop selection from the 80s. REM's "Pop Song 89".

"You'll forgive me for not taking off my shirt and doing jazz hands routines in front of the window," I said.

"Forgive you? Christ, I'll *thank* you for not removing your shirt," Garvey said.

"You know what I like about REM?" I asked him.

"What's that?"

"It's like I was saying previously. I like that REM didn't have that outwardly punk ethos, because they knew they didn't have to. They did all of their sneering with snide riffs like the one in this song. And if you didn't like it, you could fuck off for all REM cared. I liked their quiet contempt," I responded.

"So did I," Garvey obliged as he fumbled with his iPod.

"It's a man's world," he muttered.

"Eh?"

"This song. It's called "It's a Man's World", by James Brown."

"Ah. The Godfather."

"Indeed. *This* is soul music. James sounds like he's ripping the heart out of his own chest. Women frequently cover this song and it gives it an entirely different meaning. I like this version though."

I was reminded of a controversial bumper sticker that Garvey and I had seen together during one of my visits to Memphis. It read, '*so you're a feminist? Aw, that's so cute!*' I didn't remind him.

I was thrilled at the sight of my next song. I put the volume of the sound dock way up, wanting to blow the windows out of our little chalet with it. It was from a newer rock band called Rival Sons, and it was called "Pressure and Time". It was all that I asked rock and roll with which to provide me.

"I dare you not to react physiologically to this next song," I challenged Garvey as I pressed play, and immediately began to react physiologically.

"Listen to that guitar," I said. "You don't have to play all the time. You just have to play at the *right* time."

Less was indeed more. During the main riff and verses, only four notes were played in quick succession on the guitar, leaving the rest of the measure open to the drums. These four notes being played were quite possibly the same first four notes from Zeppelin's "Out on the Tiles" riff. And possibly also the same ones in Audioslave's "Show Me How To Live". But I could be wrong about that.

I turned the volume up even louder than it had been. I located my newly-opened bottle of wine, and took a drink from it. I didn't need a glass anymore. We were in gypsy territory now. Now, there was only sweet liberation to be felt.

"Gene Simmons set everyone on fire recently with his comment that rock and roll was dead. Everyone got all excited about it. But I think I know what he was talking about, and what he meant by it. I've said the same thing before, and so have a lot of other people," I said.

"I think Gene has a flair for getting people excited with comments, and I think Gene likes that," Garvey noted.

"Agreed. But what he said wasn't that outlandish, really. He was talking more about the business - the structure of what the rock business model used to look like and how it wasn't there anymore because of file sharing and so forth. He was talking about how this in turn impacts the ability for rock, and the bands who play rock, to develop any further. I think that once music became so easily accessible and the consumer was able to acquire it with such ease through sites like Napster, people began placing less value in music, and it just became more commoditized."

"Uh-huh," Garvey acknowledged.

"But I also think that rock has been *done* already, y'know? All the paths have all been forged. There won't be another Beatles or another Stones, because there can't be. There can and will be artists that serve almost as commemorations to the greats who came before them based on their influence, and that's fine. There's nothing wrong with that at all. In my opinion, pure rock and roll died in the 90s after the original version of Guns N' Roses imploded. But the *culture* of rock is what's still alive, and I have to admit that there are still a small handful of good bands out there that perpetuate that idea and embody that ethos without pretending. Rival Sons is one of those bands. It's not new, game-changing stuff, but that doesn't matter. What matters is that it's good music that pumps your blood the way rock should."

"*This has been* Brent Jensen's Rock & Roll Soapbox, *and I'm Brent Jensen. Thank you and goodnight,*" Garvey mocked.

"*Tune in next time when I expose George Michael for the soulless fraud that he is,*" I continued. "You're up, cracker."

"Okay, here's something a little different," Garvey said without looking up from the dock. "LCD Soundsystem."

"Wow, you're into this?" I asked.

"I have virtually no interest in electronic dance music, but with this song James Murphy and LCD Soundsystem force me to refrain from dismissing the genre altogether. This stuff makes me think of the best Britpop of the 80s - it's a little New Order-ish for me. Actually, a lot New Order-ish."

"I don't know this song, but LCD Soundsystem's "Daft Punk Is Playing At My House" is great too. It sounds nothing like this. I wouldn't have even guessed it was the same group," I responded.

This observation was kinda myopic on my part, but because I liked LCD Soundsystem's "Daft Punk Is Playing At My House" so much and hadn't heard any of their other music, I naturally assumed that it was their 'sound'. Most pop bands today don't have a specific 'sound', however.

Garvey's LCD Soundsystem selection was less than two minutes long, and he failed to punch out before the strains of a Jackson Browne track emanated from the sound dock. Another foul.

"Dammit. Showed my card again," Garvey said in that voice, feigning concern.

I thought we had done pretty well so far in our vigilance, given the circumstances. We were descending deeper into the nighttime now, and I wondered how many songs we had left. Also on my mind was the position of "Handbags and Glad Rags" in my list. I had been anticipating it with the wariness of the chamber that contained the bullet. As I had pulled the iPod trigger again and again, it failed to appear. But I knew it was there.

This time, depressing the forward arrow of the iPod revealed a song that instead brought glee - The Rolling Stones' "Prodigal Son", from their 1968 record *Beggars Banquet*.

"*Yes!* I love this song," I yelped. It conveyed that old blues rhythm in a very loose and pastoral context, and that's what I loved about it. The raw purity.

"I feel like Richards added a little Bo Diddley jive to this tune," I said to Garvey. "It grooves beyond what you'd expect from a typical Delta blues standard. But my favourite part is at the end. Right after Jagger's last vocal line, you can hear Richards come in and yell '*hey-y-y*' like some drunken lout who just barged into the recording session. After I noticed it the first time, I used to listen to that bit over and over again, partly because I found it hilarious, but also because I appreciated the circumstances under which the Stones would leave such a thing in. Because on the surface, it certainly didn't complement the song. If anything, the weirdness of it throws you off a bit. But that's what I love about this record and the next three that would follow it - they were all provided at a certain face value. After the pretension of the Stones' record that came out before this one, *Their Satanic Majesties Request*, any unpolished ugliness likely was seen as becoming of the Stones and what they could really do as young blues disciples."

At that moment, before Garvey would put on his next selection, Keef had emboldened me to reach for the Gibson acoustic and belt out a proper Stones standard. I picked it up, put one foot up on the arm of the chair and rested the guitar's body on my thigh, strumming an open D nice and loud.

"*I'm the ma-a-an on the mountain...,*" I worked through the chords and sang the lyrics for "Loving Cup" in a higher register at full volume, inciting a full-out rock and roll revival inside our little cabin. Garvey joined in. We yelped the song at the tops of our lungs to the heavens with open abandon, satisfied to have the opportunity to do so together.

This moment was exhilarating. One for the ages. It was at rare times like these that I felt as though I did indeed have a soul, and that it was on fire.

I fully expected to hear a knock on the door at any time advising us to kindly shut the fuck up at such a late hour. After our performance concluded, Garvey walked over to the sound dock to launch his next song. It was Jackson Browne's "The Pretender".

"Something about Browne's songs touch a nerve for me. It could be because they're tales of desperation and dysphoria in places where some might argue that the players have nothing to gripe about - the middle class suburbs. This song's a great example. It's *American Beauty* twenty five years before the movie was written. And without the explicit sexual overtones," Garvey said.

"I had always mistaken Jackson Browne for a kind of erstwhile Tom Petty," I confessed. "A sweeter, more refined version even. But I feel like this song has an early-period Billy Joel derisive flavour."

My Rolling Stones hit parade continued. Next up for me was "Sweet Virginia".

"I apologize in advance that this might be more than a double-play for Mick and Keef," I warned.

I remembered including many Stones tracks in my playlist. Whether or not I had kept them all in there remained to be seen. We sat and basked in the stripped-down glory of this song, one from their most gloriously stripped-down record, *Exile on Main Street*.

"Hear him back there?" I asked Garvey.

I was referring to Keith Richards, who could be heard singing in a higher register just behind Jagger on a lot of *Exile* tracks, most notably "Loving Cup".

"Yep. He's going to church."

"Dude, he's *in* church. He's the fucking *reverend*," I said.

"One of my favourite things about The Rolling Stones is how they gave America their own music back by introducing white American kids to the black man's blues," Garvey said.

"It's a unique concept. The Stones as white British war babies covering southern American blues by Muddy Waters, Howlin' Wolf - first getting their fellow Britons excited about it, and then invading America with their own music. Just in a package that was more favourable to young white Americans considering the times, I would think," I added.

Mick Jagger never did sing with the heartfelt beauty that someone like Smokey Robinson did, but it always seemed as though he derived a lot of pleasure from singing black songs as an antagonistic white person. Songs like "Brown Sugar" had been proof of that. This was an aspect that likely resonated strongly with white America in the early 60s.

I looked ahead on my iPod knowing that I had more Stones tunes on it, so I asked Garvey for an opportunity to remain punched in to complete the run. He approved, and the eerie malevolence of "Gimme Shelter" wafted from the dock.

"Not many bands use the fish anymore," Garvey commented.

"Guns N' Roses used it on *Appetite for Destruction*. That was the last time I've heard it."

"Do you still have yours?" Garvey asked.

"Not sure. But I wouldn't willingly throw it out. It's probably in a box somewhere in my basement."

The fish is a percussive instrument that, as far as I know, is a hollowed-out wooden carving of a fish with little ridges cut into the side of it to represent scales that make a unique sound when you drag the accompanying stick along them. That's what my fish was, anyway.

"It's hard to play. You definitely have to have a feel for it to drag the stick along the ridges in time to the beat."

"I'll stick to the shaker," Garvey responded.

"Man, you can hear the tension in the intro here. This whole song is charged with that same tension," I said.

The "Gimme Shelter" intro was a favourite part of the song. It gave me chills every time I heard it. Another favourite part was when backup singer Merry Clayton's voice cracked as she sang in the latter part of the song, testament to the electrifyingly emotive performance she gives on the track.

"Listen closely after Merry's voice gives out on that last '*murder*', and you can hear Jagger in the background say '*whoo!*'" I said to Garvey.

We poised quietly for the moment. Faintly, Jagger's endorsement was heard and Garvey smiled.

"Cool. I'd never noticed that before."

I took a pull on my bottle. "Okay, the Rolling Stones run is over," I said.

I had skipped "Moonlight Mile", and also "Loving Cup" in lieu of our little jam earlier. Hell, I could have made just a Rolling Stones playlist.

"Here's something a little left of centre," Garvey announced.

It sounded like two men talking. I didn't ask what it was, because I thought I recognized one of the men's voices. Yes, I did.

It was Bing Crosby.

"I loved this song before I knew who either of these guys were. This still moves me. I guess it helps that you only hear it at Christmas, so it doesn't get overplayed on the radio," Garvey said.

"This is fucking awesome!" I enthused.

It was David Bowie and Bing Crosby doing "The Little Drummer Boy".

"Oh man, I love this too. For the longest time I couldn't find it when I was younger, having searched every record store I could access. I had to wait for the internet to be invented in order to finally own it," I laughed.

It never felt like a Christmas carol, because Bowie's inclusion somehow eclipsed any holiday sentiment I would feel when hearing the song. I always thought there was something weirdly fascinating about the fact that David Bowie, as outlandish as he would be perceived, would be interested in playing the role of a genteel English neighbour to Bing Crosby. Was this really who he was? Or was he playing someone else? I never really knew, but I always enjoyed the grace his union with Bing Crosby would bring, even if it was fabricated. I didn't care.

My first post-Stones song was Pearl Jam's very first hit, "Alive".

"I was alone watching videos on MuchMusic at 3am back at school in the dorm TV room the first time I came across this song. It was like being hit by lightning. I had no idea who this Pearl Jam band was, but I loved this song instantly. Nirvana and the grunge movement had yet to take hold completely. This didn't sound like anything other than a good hard rock song to me, and I wanted to hear it again and again. I was obsessed with it," I explained.

"The next day I asked every other guy on my dorm floor about a band called Pearl Jam - I described the black and white video, tried to describe the song, but I didn't know what it was called. No one else had seen the video or heard the song, or of the band. I asked everyone I talked to about it to please look for me when the video happened to play next if I wasn't in the TV room. I even tried to figure out the four-hour repeating segment schedule that MuchMusic employed to cover the graveyard shift so that I could maximize my chances of seeing it again. It was 1991, years before the internet would be able to assist."

"Did you go to the record stores to look for albums by Pearl Jam?" Garvey asked.

"Yeah, of course. No luck."

"Not even at Records on Wheels?"

"Nope. No one had heard of Pearl Jam at that point. Some of the record shop guys actually looked at me strangely, like I might have been screwing with them. I wondered later if maybe they were making some kind of inference to *pearl jam* being an allusion to semen or something."

"Like *you* had?"

"The thought crossed my mind. Helluva band name. Probably a decent pickup line in some parts of Sudbury too," I answered.

"*I'm in a band. My band's name is Pearl Jam*," Garvey offered.

"*Ooooohhhh. Deep. Wait, that's gross…kinda.*" I responded, batting my eyelashes.

"*And off they go, moonlight shining brilliantly…*" Garvey trailed off. "Alright, so what ended up happening?"

"Anyway, so no one including myself saw the video for a few weeks. One of the guys was going down to Toronto one weekend, so I gave him twenty bucks and asked him to be on the lookout for any albums he might see by this band. They had to be a new band, and that likely meant they could only have one record out. Turned out they did. He brought back a CD copy of *Ten* that Sunday night, and I proceeded to ostracize myself from the rest of my dorm mates by blasting "Alive" nonstop at full volume for at least the next two weeks."

"This is The Beatles at their storytelling best," Garvey advised as he walked back to his chair from the sound dock. The morose eloquence of "Eleanor Rigby" made the walls of our chalet seem that much warmer.

"More sad and lonely characters," he continued. "My grade eight music teacher Ms. Gina King was younger, maybe in her twenties, and she used to put on music for the class to listen to when we had book-related learning to complete. That's where I first heard this. I remember her telling us to listen to the lyrics, listen to the story."

"What a great teacher," I replied.

"She was. She shared a lot of great music with us."

"You're lucky. My grade eight music teacher was a nasty old lady who yelled at us for not being able to play the recorder," I told Garvey.

As we listened to Sir Paul's musical story, I wondered if "Eleanor Rigby" might be his lyrically darkest song. It was pretty glib, but Paul didn't seem to have a dark side. He typically emoted with hope and positivity in his songs. If they made you well up, it was because of their beauty.

"All my favourite people are broken, except Macca," I said to Garvey.

I looked up to see him reclined deep into his chair, head tilted back with one Oreo cookie positioned over either eye as though he were receiving treatment at some sort of Willy Wonka spa.

"You're right," Garvey concurred as he lay motionless. "He's a bright light on an otherwise dim landscape."

"McCartney and Lennon were so polarized," I said. "From the start, Paul was the cute, likeable one and Lennon was the caustic rebel. Even when you watch their appearance on The Ed Sullivan Show, Paul looks like he's saying *'hey, let's be friends!'*."

"What's Lennon saying?" Garvey asked.

"The opposite. He looks like he's telling you that you can fuck yourself."

"All my favourite people are broken. Except Paul McCartney."

CHAPTER 17

Chasing The Dragon

"I always felt like I shouldn't be listening to this song as a young kid. It made me uncomfortable but curious at the same time," I said as Garvey and I traded notes on Canadian group Rough Trade's "High School Confidential".

"It was the first time I'd ever heard the word 'bitch' in a song lyric. I mean, I had also heard that word in Hall and Oates' "Rich Girl", but that didn't really count, y'know? It was kinda glossy, and coming from Hall & Oates it just didn't have the same bite. This one just hits you right between the eyes - first line of the song, and delivered with enough venom to make you recoil as a kid."

Garvey laughed.

"The imagery those lyrics evoked really got my attention and made me worry about what I didn't know about things like homosexuality, and what it meant for a girl to cream her jeans. It also made me want to find out who Anita Ekberg and Mamie Van Doren were," I said.

"Not to mention the idea of high school students sleeping with their school principals," Garvey added.

"Yeah! Exactly. I had heard this song right before I heard The Police's "Don't Stand So Close To Me". It was like I came into this world where all of this secret nefarious activity was just prevalent all of a sudden," I laughed.

"The things you don't know when you're a kid."

"Man, I was the most misinformed kid around. I knew nothing about any of this stuff. I once found myself in a situation with a girl where we had evaluated the efficiency of using plastic wrap and an elastic band in lieu of birth control."

"Hmmm. You *were* pretty misinformed, weren't you?" Garvey said.

"Misinformed yes, but also pretty resourceful. You're up, pal."

Garvey removed my iPod from the dock and punched in. I took a long drink from my bottle. We were only halfway through the night. His next selection was "Into the Mystic" by Van Morrison.

"This is a pretty song sung by one of our great vocal stylists. I love how Van the Man colours outside the lines when he sings. He doesn't conform to the strict structure of the song, instead he trips all over the measure and makes it his own. It's always like this beautiful dance by a drunk staggering down the street for me," Garvey described.

"He's still out there playing, isn't he? Still pissing people off?" I asked.

I only knew Morrison's music casually. I was unfortunately more familiar with his reputation for being notoriously difficult to deal with.

"Yeah, I think he's still out there."

"Was getting boozed up and falling off stages Van Morrison, or am I confusing him with David Wilcox?" I asked.

"I'm sure Van would be delighted with that comparison," Garvey answered.

"I don't care that much," I said as I got up to punch in. I saw that Sloan's "Coax Me" was next on my playlist.

"Now why wasn't Sloan as big as Foo Fighters?" I asked. "I think they could have been. These melodies are great. This band wrote some really good songs. I think they could have been much more popular." I paused for a moment. "But I like that they're not. They're like an unplugged gem, having escaped being mangled by The Fame Machine."

Garvey's turn now.

Ka-chik.

"Here's another gift from Ms. King in grade eight. One day she put on *Moving Pictures* and just let it play. I had seen kids wearing Rush t-shirts but had never heard the band's music before this. They sounded gigantic," he said as Rush's "Tom Sawyer" began.

"I had seen this album cover as a grade school kid too. I put a lot of thought into why they would make a clever play-on-words joke of it, rather than have a cover with badass imagery that was more visually representative of hard rock. Or call the album something else altogether. It's clear that the genius of Rush was lost on me. Back then I thought rock was meant to be more stereotypical and less intellectual, and I veered away from bands that indicated to me that it was anything but," I said.

Then Garvey asked me a very difficult question.

"If you could go back in time and change all of the factors that initiated your musical preferences, resulting in you *not* being a fan of the music that you were a fan of growing up, would you do it?"

Hmmm.

I sat back in my chair frozen, searching the ceiling for an answer to this question. I wasn't comfortable with the fact that the jury was out for so long; that my answer didn't come to me immediately. It should have been an immediate *no*. But I felt like there were a lot of considerations to make. After a minute or so, I offered my response.

"My answer is no, because the ramifications of these changes would be too complicated and far-reaching. My musical preferences were largely a by-product of my psychosocial environment. And that means my entire infrastructure would be subject to change." This was my answer, whether or not I wanted to believe it.

"Really? You don't want to see what's behind door number two?"

"Of course I do. Can I just have a quick look?" I asked, as though it were actually somewhere in this chalet.

"No. You would have to fully embrace it. Full embrace or nothing. No peeks."

"I'm good then. I'm too happy with the present tense and the realization that things turned out the way they did. It could have easily worked out much worse. Being the coolest kid in high school means very little later on in life," I responded.

"Suit yourself," Monty Hall said. "You're up."

Seeing behind door number two was actually the reason why I was here. But I had to do it myself. I had passed through door number two right after the first time the play button got pressed. I was happy with life as I currently experienced it, but there was still some reflecting to do.

A little more deliberation was required now to get over to the table where the sound dock was positioned, the centre of our universe here. For a fleeting moment, my mind imagined the sound dock as one of the black mysterious monoliths from Kubrick's *2001: A Space Odyssey*, holding the keys that would unlock the meaning I was trying to pull out of our time here. The absurdity of this exaggeration made me laugh out loud a little bit. The mushroom buzz was behind us now.

And now here it was in my playlist, finally. The dirge that could be my undoing. "Handbags and Glad Rags" as performed by Stereophonics was my next selection. I felt a mild anxiety as I pressed play.

Garvey had never heard this song before. I returned to my chair and sat down, gripping the neck of my half-empty wine bottle. It wouldn't help me at all.

"This is the most beautiful song I know," I said to Garvey, my voice betraying a hint of desperation as the introductory notes revealed themselves to us.

He understood that I would disappear into the music now and be alone with myself for the song's duration, somewhere else.

I sat still with my head tilted toward my shoulder, my face likely revealing my blank insularity. As the song played, it felt as though time had been suspended. My eyes focused unflinchingly on the bottle in my hand in liturgy. I was frozen in place as I submitted myself to this song, waiting for it to do it to me. I swallowed down every one of those convoluted distances that were implicit in musical emotionality, until there were none. In my blood I could feel it, that beautiful reduction, and I smiled through my tears in reverence of this sensation. When I came through the other side at the song's conclusion, I sat exposed and vulnerable in my chair.

I felt a sense of immense relief. There was no need to feel ashamed for what our emotions made of us.

Garvey walked over on his way to the table, patted my shoulder and winked with a knowing smile. We didn't have to say anything. This was a defining moment. At its fundamental core, this was the enterprise I had hoped it would be. There weren't any limits here.

After a few moments of silence, Garvey spoke.

"Michaela seldom lets me control the music when we have parties," he said, referring to his wife.

I knew why before he continued.

"She says the music I put on is always so goddamn sad, and she wonders why."

"I've always thought songs that can pull that kind of a visceral reaction from me were more genuine and sophisticated measures of what I thought real music was," I added.

Garvey nodded. "Have you ever seen any of the TED Talks?"

"Yeah, I've seen a couple of them. They're great."

TED is an organization that shares short, concise idea presentations in areas of technology, entertainment, and design (hence the acronym), as provided by leaders in their respective milieus. These talks were always informative and pretty powerful in terms of inspiration.

"Have you seen the one with Benjamin Zander, talking about the transformative power of classical music?"

"No, I haven't," I replied.

"So Zander is the conductor of the Boston Philharmonic. He talks about how most people think they can't relate to classical music, when in fact everyone can, and so he breaks the music down into single notes in front of a live audience to demonstrate. In doing this, he also talks about how notes can manipulate our emotions when they're played in a certain way, in a certain order, etcetera. That some notes make other notes 'sad'. Like for example, that C makes B sad."

"That's really interesting."

"He also talks about our innate sense of knowing which chords are 'home', based on the key of the song. Like E for example. We all instinctively know in a measure of music where the E chord should fall, where we would expect it as a resolution to the story a song tells us. Then Zander plays a familiar Chopin piece on the piano to demonstrate."

"Okay..."

"The most gripping part comes after the demonstration when, just before he plays the entire piece to prove his overall point, he asks the audience to think about someone in their lives that they had adored that was no longer there, as they followed the line of chords from B down to E. In doing this, he said, they would hear everything that Chopin was trying to say," Garvey explained.

I listened intently, riveted by this.

"So after he plays the whole thing, the audience gives him a standing ovation. Some people are moved to tears."

"Incredible," I said.

"I love that we all know where we want the music to go, that the seemingly correct next note is not really all that subjective. We all know what the music *wants* to do, and a good composer knows this and extends those natural musical resolutions so that a story can be told," Garvey enthused.

"And reduces us at the same time," I added.

This was the very aspect of music that I was so completely obsessed with, and always had been.

⁘

Garvey's next selection was "Crazy" by Patsy Cline. Our playlists continued their serpentine relationship, undulating with one other and then moving away for a time. This was definitely away.

"Cline's voice is clarion clear, and so goddamn powerful. Patsy Cline could sing the phone book. And Willie Nelson wrote this song, before he was *Willie Nelson*," Garvey said.

As I listened to this song, I found it interesting how Garvey and I could see so much in these songs that the other did not. It was the power of nostalgia and sentimental positioning stirring an interest to dig deeper. Sentimentality was the motivational force in experiencing songs on an entirely unique plane.

"You're up, pal," Garvey advised.

My selection would slingshot us from the 60s back into the new millennium. It was Sufjan Stevens' "Casimir Pulaski Day". I punched in and walked over to the fireplace to renew the roar of the fire.

"Who's this?" Garvey asked.

"Sufjan Stevens. Ever heard of him?"

"No, I don't think so. But I like this."

"A friend of mine made a mix CD for me a while back with this song on it, and I loved it. It's breezy singer-songwriter folk, with some unique tweaks. The lyrics are really clever too. I liked it so much that I went out and bought the CD thinking that based on the quality of this song, there had to be other similar sounding songs."

"I know where this is going."

"Well, I don't ever expect a perfect record, y'know? I figure there's bound to be one or two, or even four clunkers on most albums. And that's fine. As long as there are at least three other songs on it that I enjoy, I'll buy the record."

"And?"

"Bust. The name of the record should have been my first clue. It's called *Sufjan Stevens Invites You To: Come On Feel the Illinoise*, and the cover features Superman, Al Capone, and a goat in cartoon imagery."

"Sounds nice," Garvey exhaled.

"The album is one of those eccentric, experimental instrumentation affairs that I can't identify with. This song, "Casimir Pulaski Day", is a red herring. It sounds nothing like anything else on the record. I hate when that happens. I bought it in 2005, and I've consulted iTunes for audio samples before buying an artist's entire album ever since."

"This is a good tune though," Garvey replied after he poured himself a glass of white wine and made his way toward the sound dock. It had to be well into the morning now.

"This is a very special song for me," he said quietly. I didn't recognize it.

"What is it?"

"It's called "Stardust" by Willie Nelson. I love Willie's voice. It's delicate and unique, and he breathes new life into these old standards. It's a gorgeous record. This is nighttime listening, with a drink in hand. Probably wine."

I nodded in silence.

"My mom used to stay up late in her nightgown, smoking cigarettes at the dining room table with a glass of warm brandy, this record turned up loud and the lights turned low."

His description conjured a crystalline image for my mind to see. I had been a dinner guest seated at that very table in his parents' home. I could see emotion in Garvey's face through the hazy glow cast from the fireplace.

"This song brings me back there. Chokes me up a bit," Garvey spoke, his voice cracking in his throat.

I sent a brave smile over to my friend, and felt a pang of emotion myself as we looked at each other. There was a sense of release in what we were doing here, that we could share all of this together.

U2's "Red Hill Mining Town" was my next song. As a teenager, I had always forced allusive connections from songs that seemed to make them available to me, even if the song's specific message had nothing to do with my own situation. If the music was right, and powerful enough, I looked to the lyrics. And if there was even a fleeting lyrical connection to whatever my situation was, I placed myself inside it. And "Red Hill Mining Town", as beautiful and damned as it was, immediately obliged me in my efforts back then.

"Great pick," Garvey said.

"I really looked for connectivity in this song as a kid growing up in a small town, but I didn't know at the time that it had more of a political bent. Nonetheless, it was fragile just like I was. U2 wasn't my music as a teenager, and I still feel like it means more to other people than it does to me. But this song was compelling enough to steal me away for a while. *Joshua Tree* is a brilliant album. It's a proper masterpiece," I said.

We sat silently, receiving this music as it filled the room.

"Y'know, you have to give yourself to that *thing*, the way Bono does with "Red Hill Mining Town". Good songs are the product of a musician giving themselves to that thing, chasing that dragon," Garvey responded.

"Couldn't agree more," I said as I looked out the window into the blackness of the woods. This is what we were doing out here, secluded up in the mountains - giving ourselves to this thing the best we knew how at this point in our lives.

CHAPTER 18

Uncracked Jack

Fleetwood Mac's "Dreams" was next up for Garvey.
"I love this song for Mick Fleetwood's drums as much as anything. They're delicate. He's probably using brushes. And then he hits that crash cymbal heading into the chorus and it just pops. Listen - see?" Garvey said as he mimed on his own imaginary kit.

"He delays it somewhat there," I noted. "Hits the cymbal just a little after you'd expect it."

Garvey nodded with a smile. "Exactly."

"I always think about "Go Your Own Way" when I think about Mick Fleetwood," I went on. "You can hear the cocaine in the drum tracks. Mick Fleetwood is just this snare drum colossus in that song."

The mood inside our chalet was sedate. I opened another bottle and a bag of Ruffles. It was still dark outside, but it couldn't be for much longer. We'd listened to a lot of music up to this point. I looked across the room at Garvey, eyes closed and slowly rolling his head from side to side against the back of his chair, back and forth, a look of quiet contentment on his face as Fleetwood Mac played on. That was it. That was the same peace I wanted. I'd never quite been able to feel that. I wondered if that peace would ever come to me.

"How many songs you got left?" Garvey asked.

"A few. Not many more, probably. You?"

"Looks like about fifty more."

"Whatever. Here's a little number for you," I said as I punched in and played Wall of Voodoo's "Mexican Radio".

"Whoa!" Garvey said, his surprised reaction blunted somewhat by the late hour. "You like this?"

"I love this. The first time I heard it was on *American Bandstand*. I tuned in every Saturday at one o'clock in the afternoon. This song was bizarre. It had this charismatic snarkiness to it that I'd always liked."

"You want snark?" Garvey asked as he called up his next song following the conclusion of "Mexican Radio". "Here's some snark for you. This is The Who's "Young Man Blues", the band at their most powerful. Pete Townshend's tone at Leeds is perfect – he's playing a Gibson SG Special with P90 pickups through a Hiwatt amp," he explained.

"This is *Live at Leeds*?"

"Damn straight, motherfucker."

"I never really got into The Who. There was a guy I knew in high school who absolutely worshipped The Who, and yet he didn't like any other of the bands from that era - The Kinks, Stones, nothing. I was always very suspicious of that. I wondered if for some peculiar reason he was just claiming to like The Who to seek attention, but he had all the records and everything. And liking things ironically wasn't in style yet. Other than The Who, he liked what every other person who secretly hated music liked at that time - INXS and George Michael," I said.

"Now I can see where your George Michael hostility is coming from," Garvey said.

"George Michael's motivation in manipulating the feelings of his fans was too blatantly obvious. That's where it comes from, amigo."

"Lay down on the couch, and tell me about your mother," Garvey cracked.

"Nah. I'm going to tell you about this next song instead."

I pulled Garvey's iPod out of the dock and inserted my own. "I did like that Who track, by the way," I said. "I'll be picking that up for sure."

"Alright. Lay it on me, brother," Garvey said as he leaned back in his chair.

My next song was "Ball and Biscuit" by The White Stripes. That glorious guitar tone crunched its way out of the dock and Garvey's eyebrows rose as much as they could at this point.

"Very nice," he said.

"I really believed in this song. The first time I heard it, it almost felt like rock was being resurrected. It was loose and the time was sloppy, plodding on with that slow and deliberate force. You could hear the ache of the old equipment in Jack White's music. It was real, and I was enthralled. Technology had seemingly choked rock and roll out of the landscape around that time, with the rise of techno raves and people like DJ Tiesto or whatever his name is. It seemed more about gadgetry than music. Pure musical essence was just…gone. Going to see acts like Skrillex just seemed like going to some big drug party, the music replaced with just this one continually long noise. I don't know if those DJ-based 'concerts' would be any fun without drugs. It was like, '*hey, come and watch me push buttons on my laptop!*'"

Garvey nodded.

"But I do like that this stuff seems to force people like Jack White, a guy who used analog equipment before it was retro-chic, to go even further back in time and do things like put Neil Young in one of those vinyl recording boxes from the 40s. Did you see them do that on Jimmy Fallon?"

"Yeah, I heard about it. What was that thing?" Garvey asked.

"It's called a Voice-O-Graph, it's about the size of a telephone booth. You go in and record your song, and it's recorded directly to vinyl on the spot. Neil Young demonstrated it on Fallon. He went in and played an old folk song on his acoustic, and a minute later there was the vinyl record, complete with that old classic sound."

"That's great."

"It's available for use to the public at Third Man Records in Nashville. It wasn't there the last time I was, but when I'm back next summer I think I'm going to give it a go," I told Garvey.

"The world needs more Jack Whites," Garvey responded.

"Indeed. What's next, dude?"

Garvey conferred with his iPod. "U2 appears to be next."

"Is this "Bad?"," I asked.

"Yep. Fucking U2, man," Garvey said as he plopped down into his chair. "Seemingly simple riffs, but not at all simple. And lyrics that are sooooo heavy."

The Edge's guitar combined with Bono's vocals in a creamy meditation that perfectly suited the atmosphere in our chalet at that moment. I wanted to play the song over and over again. As much as the formality of our exercise was becoming sloppier as time went on, we refrained from deviation for the most part. I picked up my iPod and punched in.

"I would be remiss if I didn't include some of this in my playlist," I said as I pressed play.

"Is this Peabo Bryson?" Garvey said.

I started laughing.

"*Peabo Bryson*!? What?!" I yelled through my laughter. "Where the hell did *that* come from?"

"What is it then?"

"It's Whitesnake. "Love Ain't No Stranger"," I replied.

"Oh, Christ."

"You said there would be no judgment!"

Garvey smirked, but just a very slight, unenthusiastic smirk. He was all business when the Whitesnake was playing. Hated it.

"Come on, man. This is the last really good Whitesnake record. Nice British bluesy hard rock with just the right amount of attitude. The next record was out of control," I said.

"You mean the one with the song whose video had Tawny Kitaen trying to fit a Jaguar into her vagina?"

"Yeah, that's the one. That song was called "Here I Go Again"," I responded.

"Indeed," Garvey deadpanned.

"This song fills me with the joy of my memories of being an unjaded, thrill seeking kid. I used to love David Coverdale during this period. He was badass before America ate him up, man. My favourite part of this song is right at the end, right here, coming up…"

Coverdale's hushed voice slowly repeated the last line of the chorus unaccompanied one final time. *I ain't no stranger-rr-rr-rr…*

"Ah. Providence," I said quietly. It meant absolutely nothing to Garvey.

I wondered at that moment about how much he was taking away from my playlist, if anything. He got up to punch in as I headed for the bathroom. I could hear what vaguely sounded like a live version of Neil Young's "Helpless" being played.

"Is this live?" I asked.

"It's from *The Last Waltz*," Garvey yelled back. After I returned to my chair, he continued to explain his selection.

"This is proof positive that you only need three chords and the truth. But it certainly doesn't hurt to have Robbie Robertson, Eric Clapton, and Joni Mitchell playing behind you. This particular version transcends itself," Garvey said.

"I think I just heard Joni in there somewhere," I said.

It was funny how we used the given names of the musicians we felt an affinity for in our discussions, and the surnames of those we did not. The exception was when I used 'Cov' to describe David Coverdale a few minutes before. That meant special affinity. I really dug Cov.

"I still don't understand why everyone made such a big deal of Eric Clapton's playing. I think he's overrated," I said.

"That's sacrilege," Garvey replied.

"Why? How is he as good as a Jeff Beck or a Jimmy Page? I just don't hear it. I don't mind saying that I don't think he's a special guitar player, at all. He's medium talent. Good player, nothing extraordinary."

I thought back to the story I'd heard about Bill Murray calling Chevy Chase 'medium talent' backstage in front of the other *Saturday Night Live* cast members during one of their many dustups. It was regarded by some who witnessed it as the most cutting thing that Bill Murray could have said to Chevy Chase. I didn't need to be that cutting, the comment just came out. I just didn't understand all the hype.

"You going to put that in your book?" Garvey asked.

"Yeah, probably."

"Then you can put me down as being in disagreement. I would never go on record as saying that Clapton is an average guitar player."

"I haven't heard anything that would lead me to believe that he's not," I expressed.

"We can agree to disagree on that."

"Agreed," I said with a smile. "I hope my next song is a Van Halen song."

It was not. It was "Daydream Believer" by The Monkees.

"Man, this is great. This is just a perfect, timeless pop progenitor. It was between this song and "Happy Together" by The Turtles for inclusion in my playlist. I also considered David Cassidy's "I Think I Love You", but it's not better than this. "Happy Together" is close, but this chorus is sublime. I feel it more," I explained.

"I do like this. I like the purity of this," Garvey agreed.

"It's beautiful music, maybe made a little bit more beautiful by its implied distance."

"You know what else is beautiful?"

I took a sip of scotch from my glass. I don't drink that stuff out of the bottle.

"What else is beautiful?" I asked.

"The Rolling Fucking Stones," Garvey shouted like a demented preacher as he pressed play to launch the second pass of "Can't You Hear Me Knocking", the only song that held the distinction of appearing in both our playlists. I thought it was great, and maybe just a bit unlikely, that only one song did.

"This was among the greatest guitar tones ever recorded. And Mick Taylor is the best guitar player ever to have been in the Rolling Stones," Garvey said.

"Better than Clapton," I answered.

Garvey shook his head in disgust. "You're up, you disrespectful monster."

I laughed as I advanced to my next song, "Julia" from The Beatles.

"This album was my introduction to The Beatles. A guy I used to hang out with dorm in my sophomore year smoked a lot of dope, and around that time I felt as though I was at a crossroads in my life. I didn't have a lot of direction, and I had no idea where I was headed. No real plan. I was just kinda floating. It was that time in your life when you think that you're uniquely smarter than everyone else and can't be told anything, y'know?"

"Oh yeah," Garvey replied.

"I was twenty years old, and I was out of my mind. This guy in dorm was teaching me how to play guitar. I was really anxious to learn, and so I fell into the whole scene and spent pretty much my entire second year levitating in his smoky little room, and side two of *The White Album* playing over and over again. I always focused on "Julia" - it seemed so mysterious and ethereal. It just really reached out to me at that time. Most of that year was completely lost. There were parties all the time; massive parties that involved the whole dorm, hundreds of young wasted people. We were all looking for the same things.

"So one night this guy and I found ourselves trapped on the inside of his room because there was a Grey Cup keg party happening, and the whole floor of our dorm was jammed with people, hallways and all. We were drinking in there and eventually had to relieve ourselves, so finally he went in an empty Jack Daniel's bottle that was on the floor. He was messed up, and he thought it would be funny to put some instant coffee in it to tint the colour and make it look more like whiskey and less like someone's urine. Then he put it back on the shelf where it was before we drank it, and we both had a good laugh because it looked just like whiskey."

"And where did *you* relieve yourself?" Garvey asked.

"I went out the window."

"From eleven floors up?"

"Yeah. I had to. There were no other empty bottles in the room. Seemed perfectly reasonable at the time, you know."

Garvey reared his back in laughter. He was familiar with all of the stupidity from those days.

"So over the course of this party we could hear people outside over the loud music banging up against the door, and then we heard the voice of this geeky frosh who lived with us. He was pounding on the door and yelling our names, asking to be let in. We didn't want the room to get flooded with all these people, so we didn't answer. He left but then he came back a few times, and he was insistent on getting into the room. He knew we were in there. So eventually, we let him in."

"Okay…"

"Now this guy *never* had any booze of his own. No one really had any money back then, but this guy had a reputation for always sponging party favours from everyone else. And it wasn't like anyone really even liked him at all. He was mostly an asshole who used to steal everyone else's booze. So at one point he looks up to the shelf and says to us through his stupid grin, '*uncracked bottle of Jack up there, I see*'. Without speaking, we both knew what would happen next."

"No…"

"Oh yes. We provided a can of Coke and reached up for the bottle of coffee piss, and prepared a nice stiff drink for him like the good hosts that we were. And he drank it. And then he drank another one."

Garvey made a face.

"Christ, are you kidding?"

"No. He was drunk and very obnoxious, trying to impress a couple of upper year guys. The guy was a jackass."

"Did you ever tell him?"

"I don't remember how that all played out. I think someone else eventually told him. He laughed it off."

"Jesus," Garvey said.

"There were a lot of stories like that one from that year. It was messy. But two good things came of it - I learned how to play guitar, and I discovered *The White Album*."

CHAPTER 19

Leaving For Good

"Everything Muddy Waters did was heavy. This is a song like most of his others - it's about being the biggest, baddest motherfucker on the block," Garvey said of his next song, Muddy Waters' "Rollin' Stone".

"This is where The Rolling Stones got their name, no?" I asked.

"I think so, yeah."

"I had heard that in the early days before the band played their first gig, Brian Jones was on the phone with a gig booker. When the booker asked Jones for the band name, Jones looked down at a pile of records and saw Muddy Waters' "Rollin' Stone" and replied that his band was called The Rollin' Stones."

"Ah," Garvey intoned.

"It's crazy to think that Brian Jones was actually the guy who put that band together, isn't it? He was actually the band's leader in the beginning, the guy who got them out there while Jagger was scared to death of live audiences and chugged pints before going on when they were playing the pubs. But as Jagger and Keef got some songs together, they rose up against his leadership and pushed him out."

"And Jones just went into a downward drug-addled spiral and lost everything. Never recovered."

"Troubling story," I said.

"Alright, what else you got for me?" Garvey took a gulp from his glass.

"Some late-period Bowie."

"Eh? And what would this be? Would it be Tin Machine maybe?" Garvey questioned, referencing Bowie's heavier late 80s and early 90s Pixies-ish band, during which Bowie actually had a beard.

"No, but I need to revisit that Tin Machine stuff actually, come to think of it," I responded. "This song is from an album called *Heathen* that Bowie released much later, around 2000 or so. The track is called "Slow Burn"," I said as I pressed play.

"This song always gets me. The blood of it. It's another testament to Bowie's genius - the fact that this is far from a sad ballad, yet the chorus is so poignant and grief-stricken that Bowie could make you cry just with his vocal delivery, sung in that gorgeously doomed vibrato. I don't know that anyone was ever more prophetic in revealing the disappointments of life than David Bowie. He always operated on a much higher level, way ahead of the curve, with an ease that made his genius look so simple."

"Powerful stuff," Garvey complied after the song ended, as he rose to reveal his next selection. It was Led Zeppelin's "What Is and What Should Never Be". He remained standing as he talked.

"This is a great Zeppelin song, which means it's more like an opera with multiple acts. At the breakdown here, when Jimmy's guitar pans from left to right and back again, it's one of those unique moments that reminds us how special Led Zeppelin songs are. Their songs had such depth. Each one is like a really great book," he said.

"Yeah. I practically could have thrown a dart at Zeppelin's catalogue for inclusions in my playlist. Their catalogue is just so rich with all sorts of musical flavours, from "Communication Breakdown" to "Hot Dog". Plenty of special songs in there."

The drink was really exaggerating my commentary now. I wasn't typically so effusive, particularly when it came to Zeppelin's "Hot Dog".

"You're up, pally," Garvey said.

My next song coaxed a smile from his lips. It was The Eagles' "I Can't Tell You Why".

"I never really cared much for The Eagles, but this song always slipped under my skin when I heard it. It starts out sinister but then it has this kind of arcane quality about it, like some slow secret, in a gentler way that none of the other Eagles songs had. Eagles songs always seemed too obvious to me. I always wondered if the distinguishing factor here was the Timothy B. Schmit vocal. That falsetto just makes it more palatable somehow, more vulnerable," I said.

"The Eagles' music was too obvious for you?"

"Wasn't it? What about "Take It Easy"? And it's hard to imagine a less inspired band name than The Eagles," I responded.

"Not really," Garvey said. "What about The Animals?"

I stared at the floor, then shrugged. We could do this all night.

"Alright, fair enough. We can give credit to The Eagles for at least being creative enough to name themselves after a specific *type* of animal. You're up, you cantankerous bastard," I responded.

"Me?!?! Christ, man. Come on," Garvey warbled as he sorted his next selection. I recognized Joe Strummer's sneer under what sounded like a galloping Johnny Cash-style snare drum riff. I thought it was him, at least.

"Clash?"

"Yep. Another great rock song that seems simple but is surprisingly tough to play. One of my favourite songs from one of favourite bands," Garvey said.

I didn't know The Clash's material beyond stuff like "Rock the Casbah".

"I think this is the first Clash song I've heard that renders that actual Sex Pistols punk deployment. It sounds like the drummer deliberately slowed down to play behind the beat after that skiffle-ish drum riff that he started the song with. Or maybe he just got tired after all that," I mocked.

It was late. I didn't have much left. Humour would come at a premium now, if it would come at all. We had to be close to the end at this point. I could see through the window that the blackness was receding. The sun was coming up.

Garvey ignored my wisecracking. "This is a time capsule quality rock song."

I accepted this claim, whether or not I agreed.

Everything in this room was governed by slower motion now. I heard a good portion of the beginning of Garvey's next song before he could get to the sound dock to suppress it.

"What's that?" I asked. "Let it play, I like this."

"It's Gillian Welch. The song is "Elvis Presley Blues"," Garvey said as he turned to sit back down.

"This is one of the most beautiful songs I've ever heard. I love everything Welch does. She's one of those artists that everybody in Nashville knows, but few people know outside of Nashville. The voice, the sparse instrumentation are great, but the lyrics...damn, I wish I could write lyrics like that. It's Elvis Presley as prophet, who gave away everything he had, and everything he was, to change the world. Then he laid down and died, and was grateful for the rest. Just like John Henry did. Brilliant."

"This is brilliant," I enthused. "I love this."

What an unexpectedly beautiful juncture this was, suddenly.

I sat quietly as this song hypnotized me with its delicate darkness. I felt that rarified excitement of being exposed to compelling music for the first time. This would be Garvey's last number. His playlist had been exhausted. With this song, my pusher had provided me with one last splendid and powerful score, one I could inject into myself and have run through my blood. One that, even if only for the four minutes or so of its duration, could still the maelstrom that swirled in my head.

As we approached the close of our aural Show & Tell enterprise here, I acknowledged the semblance of this undertaking to the two of us making a big, grandiose mixtape for each other. And we both knew that you only make mixtapes for other people to a certain degree. Really, you mostly make them for yourself.

I stood and looked at my playlist. I was also down to my very last song now.

As I pressed play for the final time here, a live version of Sheryl Crow's "Leaving Las Vegas" flooded the room. The live version was in this playlist, because Sheryl evoked so much more pathos when she played this song live.

I stared at the planks that formed the floor of our dimly lit chalet, searching for the words.

"This song was playing on the car radio as I backed out of my mom's driveway and left home for Toronto in January 1995 to start a brand new life. I lived in that house on Tudhope Street since I had been a young kid. It was where I had done most of my growing up. I'd left home for long stretches of school several times before but I had always come back, and this place had been my home until this moment. My mom stood on the porch waving goodbye just outside the door. She had done this every time

I left before, waving and mustering a weak but brave smile. This time, as the car went into drive and began to move away, I looked back at her and noticed that there was no smile, and that she was crying as she waved good-bye. She had never, ever done that before. But we both knew I wouldn't be back this time. As I drove away Sheryl so serendipitously emoted that line about taking a losing hand and making it win, and that memory has always stayed with me like some lonely talisman from that day. That's what I left home to do, though I had no idea it would be that hard. But the depression I felt was lent a certain poignancy by this song. It did what every sad song should do - it dignified an otherwise unfortunate emotion," I told Garvey.

With that, I looked up at my friend, unable to do anything but smile a weak yet brave smile at him. And from his chair across the room, he smiled one back.

Afterword

After I returned home from being out there, I thought some more about what I had done.

The superficial intention of the trip was to isolate those special songs that made me feel something, and celebrate them. I wanted to get closer to them, along with one of my best friends who would be doing the same thing as a fellow music fanatic. In doing so, it would bring us closer together too. He was someone I'd always respected highly.

So, not a bad forum for a bit of some self-examination. We would share our most personal musical emblems with each other and if we were being honest about it, which we were, we would share significant pieces of ourselves at the same time. And I didn't take this sort of thing lightly. Among its many other applications, music may have been something I used to hide behind. Now I would find myself having to face up to considerations like these directly. To pull back the curtain on my emotional nebulae was a personal and less than comfortable proposition.

Like Mike Tyson said, everyone has a plan until they get hit in the mouth. When I was out there, I started to feel uncertain about what I was looking for. I was overthinking the whole thing. Trying to ensure that I pulled something quantifiable out of the experience. Though I hadn't intended it, I realized early on that Garvey would serve as an inadvertent control group, or at least as a measuring stick as someone I respected, against my examination of this music that controlled my feelings. I didn't necessarily expect for this to happen, but it did.

I considered the envy I might feel for the peace Garvey already seemed to have where his favourite music was concerned. He was unapologetic for his love of songs that were decidedly uncool. Like Carole King's "Natural Woman", for example. He'd always been that way, and I admired it. It might have even put me on my heels a bit out there.

I had been a bit uneasy about what my songs might say about me as a person. The real premise behind this exercise was to try to understand the reasons behind my fascination with this music so I could work out any uneasiness, even if it meant going to some ugly places to do so. Maybe it would bring some sort of peace, maybe like the peace Garvey had.

It was clear that most of the songs in my playlist fell under a small number of easily defined groupings. There were songs that represented happiness, relaxation, and nostalgia. Nothing unusual about that. But the grouping in my playlist containing the most songs was also the one that elicited the most visceral responses - these were the slow, saddish songs. This stuff was what I wanted to look at. It was obvious why anyone would like happy, relaxing songs. That was normal; there was no point in looking further into why I would be interested in things that represent happiness. It would be worthwhile to look into a predilection for sadness, however.

We all have our own personal truths. Some people worship gods and believe in religion. Some believe in karma or other rules of the universe related to some oblique form of spiritualism. I'd lived most of my life in the shadow of a Greek tragedy of sorts. I used to believe that there would always be some price to pay related to some tragic flaw. There was a consistent guilt that needed to be felt from a very young age.

From that age, music served as a pacifier. Sad, tragic songs seemed like logical sources of investment for my feelings. I remember experiencing a mild form of contentment when I heard the song "Send in the Clowns" for the first time as a really young kid. I felt a strange gratification in investing my emotions in this song. A satisfying smoothing of all of the jagged edges. And this would establish a pattern that made sad songs extraordinarily attractive to me as I progressed through my life. They converted fragility and loneliness into a peculiar form of entertainment. They fashioned strengths from weaknesses. As I was growing up, these songs allowed me to access melancholy as a sort of quiet vindication. But there was confusion, of course. For a while I didn't know if these songs made the holes in my heart, or filled them.

The yin to this yang was hard rock and heavy metal. My fascination with this stuff while I was growing up was partly attributable to the flashy stimulus it provided to a kid with little access to any stimulus at all. But the real reasons for the emotional investment were the aggression and power themes. I felt like it provided me with a greater semblance of control. When I heard the opening guitar riffs of my favourite metal songs, it was like a sort of exorcism. I felt like these songs lifted me right off of the ground. The elevation that these songs provided actually overcompensated for my vulnerabilities. Springsteen wasn't aggressive enough. Zeppelin wasn't aggressive enough, nor was Deep Purple. It had to be Iron Maiden. Early Metallica.

So there it was. Melancholic songs were my emotional vice, offset by hard rock and metal. They worked together symbiotically to strive for my best possible balance, much in the same way that cocaine and Quaaludes did for junkies. And I was certainly an addict.

This all made more sense to me when I considered it through the lens of a playlist. Before this little meditation in the mountains, I didn't realize why I found a song like KISS' "Sure Know Something" so compelling. But the reason was because it was the first song I had ever heard that accommodated both my emotional joneses. When I was twelve and hyper-impressionable, this song sounded like it was able to transmute loneliness into aggression, and this set the stage for my metal fixation later on as a teenager. "Sure Know Something" suggested to my childhood mind that aggression could be a suitable alternative to loneliness for me. This song fused melancholy with aggression at a critical time in my youth, and whether that was cool or uncool, it didn't matter. The impacts were long lasting. It may seem a bit ridiculous, but…most of these things are.

We don't ask for this stuff to play out the way it does. These personal truths slither around underneath all the layers some of us put in place to protect our emotional vulnerabilities. Our individual playlists will tell some pretty interesting stories if we let them.

Our songs explain who we are to ourselves. We can't choose. The peace comes in accepting this.

Acknowledgements

I'd like to express my sincere thanks to the following individuals:

Fred Garvin, my partner in crime. I'm ready to do it again anytime you are.

Proper Tennessean and quality human being Jamie Blaine, for your incredible support and for consistently telling it like it is. This book is better as a result of your input.

Fellow scribes Joel McIver, 'Uncle' Joe Daly, Martin Popoff, Jon Wiederhorn, and Neil Daniels for your insight, assistance, promotion, and kind words.

My publicist Sam Gibson, for successfully stickhandling through some tricky terrain.

My awesome wife and best pal Alison, for always being there.

The wheel turns. It turns slowly, but it does turn. These people keep it turning, and they deserve my gratitude for having contributed in some form or another: Bryan Sloss, Christopher 'The Pink Chief' Long, Lee 'Beef' Eckley, Trevor 'T-Bone' Dennis, Thomas Doyle, Derek Williamson at Thunder Bay Arena Rock, Jenny and Jamie Wylie, Kim Mitchell, my pally from the valley Ian O'Malley and his lovely bride Debbie, Dodie Dotson Woodard, Nicholas Walsh, Charles & Lissa Knight, Brad Jemmett, Carine Engelbrecht at Readers' Favorite, Gavin DeGraw, Dolly Meadowcroft, Michael Holmes at ECW Press, Craig and Jennifer Sutoski, Sloane Stephenson, John and Penny Belton, Brooke Dennis, The Baileys, Danko Jones, Crystal Marie,

BRENT JENSEN

Ryan Dunford, Ron Robichaud, Jeff Woods, Phil Collen, Andrea Chase Cormier, Steve and Melissa Flemming, Rob Mitchell, Cedarbrook Trail, Chapters Indigo, and that cat lady on Goodreads - you've helped me in spite of yourself.

About The Author

Brent Jensen is a Canadian freelance writer and music critic who lives in the Toronto area. In addition to *All My Favourite People Are Broken*, he is also the author of *No Sleep 'Til Sudbury: Adventures in 80s Hard Rock and Heavy Metal Deconstruction* (Edwards Press, 2012), in which he reflects on his teenage life and the critical role music played as a means to make sense of the world that surrounded him as he navigated the challenges of small town adolescence. As Jensen puts it, "It's the rock and roll book I could never find in the bookstore".

In 2014 Jensen released his second title, *Leftover People: A Journey Through Post-Rock & Roll America* (Edwards Press, 2014), taking his readers along on a promotional book tour of the southeastern United States in support of *No Sleep 'Til Sudbury*. The result is a unique balance of lawless hilarity and darkened introspection.

Jensen maintains Facebook and Twitter pages to network with his friends and readers, and can be reached at nosleeptilsudbury@yahoo.ca.

Made in the USA
Columbia, SC
19 January 2018